Managing Portfolios of Change with MSP™ for Programmes and PRINCE2™ for Projects

London: TSO

TSO
information & publishing solutions

Published by TSO (The Stationery Office) and available from:

Online
www.tsoshop.co.uk

Mail, Telephone, Fax & E-mail
TSO
PO Box 29, Norwich, NR3 1GN
Telephone orders/General enquiries: 0870 600 5522
Fax orders: 0870 600 5533
E-mail: customer.services@tso.co.uk
Textphone 0870 240 3701

TSO Shops
16 Arthur Street, Belfast BT1 4GD
028 9023 8451 Fax 028 9023 5401
71 Lothian Road, Edinburgh EH3 9AZ
0870 606 5566 Fax 0870 606 5588

TSO@Blackwell and other Accredited Agents

The information contained in this publication is believed to be correct at the time of manufacture. Whilst care has been taken to ensure that the information is accurate, the publisher can accept no responsibility for any errors or omissions or for changes to the details given.

Chris Venning has asserted his moral rights under the Copyright, Designs and Patents Act 1988, to be identified as the author of this work.

MSP™ is a Trade Mark of the Office of Government Commerce
PRINCE2™ is a Trade Mark of the Office of Government Commerce
The Swirl logo™ is a Trade Mark of the Office of Government Commerce
The PRINCE2 Cityscape logo™ is a Trade Mark of the Office of Government Commerce in the United Kingdom and other countries
PRINCE® is a Registered Trade Mark of the Office of Government Commerce in the United Kingdom and other countries

A CIP catalogue record for this book is available from the British Library
A Library of Congress CIP catalogue record has been applied for

First published 2007

ISBN 9780113310753

Printed in the United Kingdom by The Stationery Office, London

N5689991 c13 12/07

Contents

List of figures

List of tables

Acknowledgements

ABOUT THE AUTHOR

Chris Venning, MSP author, specializes in delivering and rescuing complex, large-scale change, and ensuring the ownership, visibility and control across portfolios and programmes to do this. Formerly Group Head of Change Governance at Barclays, Chris has delivered transformational change in organizations including NatWest, Hitachi Europe, Cable & Wireless and the Department for Transport.

REVIEWERS

Andrew Schuster, Department of Health

Helen Goulding, Audit Commission

Colin Bartle-Tubbs, Serco Group

Bruce McNaugton, Customer Driven Solutions Limited

Mike Cashman, Actalpha Delta Ltd

Russell Macdonald, The Macdonald Craven Partnership Limited

Stefan M R Plocki, PSMS South West Limited

Steve Boronski, Remarc Professional Development

Wendy Mills, The Law Society

Carol Bartlett, Amicar Consulting

Colin Daysh, BT Ireland

Fraser Fergusson, NHS National Services Scotland

Lynn Godfrey, HM Revenue & Customs

John McCain, HM Revenue & Customs

The author would like to thank the Reviewing Team for their common sense, perceptivity and helpful comments, and particularly Zoe Peden for her support and understanding.

MATURITY MARK

The TSO maturity mark on the back cover will help you decide if this publication is positioned at the appropriate level for your requirements and provide a route map to progress with embedding OGC guidance. This publication, *Managing Portfolios of Change with MSP for Programmes and PRINCE2 for Projects*, is level 5.

Level 5 is Optimizing (process improvement) – deliberate process optimization/improvement.

For more information on the TSO maturity mark and how it can help you, please visit www.best-management-practice.com

Introduction 1

1 Introduction

This book is aimed at those responsible for designing and managing portfolios and programmes of change. Within this, the book provides pragmatic approaches for integrating programmes run under MSP (Managing Successful Programmes) with projects run under PRINCE2 (PRojects IN Controlled Environments). This book will therefore also be of interest to professionals and people working in/for organizations that have or will adopt MSP and PRINCE2.

There are a number of drivers and requests that have resulted in this book:

- Portfolio management, particularly for large-scale, complex change, is increasingly becoming established as the interface between the organizational ownership and delivery of that change. In this model, portfolios of change are composed of programmes (themselves composed of projects) and stand-alone projects.
- PRINCE2 is the most established project management methodology in the world, and MSP is establishing for itself a similar status among programme management methodologies. Although both are owned by the OGC, the two methods have not been hitherto designed with integration as a core feature.
- Integrating MSP and PRINCE2 is a challenge that many organizations are facing. When the organization also operates a portfolio-driven model of managing change, the challenges are greater. How MSP and PRINCE2 will operate together in a portfolio environment is a challenge that has not been broadly faced.

The book gives practical and pragmatic advice on how to integrate MSP and PRINCE2 within a cohesive portfolio-driven framework that:

- Reinforces the best-practice principles of both MSP and PRINCE2
- Gives the strategic alignment and organizational ownership of good portfolio management.

The guide explains the principles of portfolio management and provides practical advice on setting up a portfolio management function. The main audience for this guide will be the teams responsible for coordinating programmes and projects, particularly those providing support for investment decisions and reporting on progress to the management (or portfolio) board. A working knowledge of programme and project management control and progress reporting is assumed.

1.1 WHAT IS PORTFOLIO MANAGEMENT?

Portfolio management is the corporate, strategic-level process for coordinating successful delivery across an organization's entire set of programmes and projects. The total set of programmes and projects within an organization is known as the 'portfolio' and represents the complete picture of the organization's commitment of programme and project resources and investment to deliver its strategic objectives.

There is a clear distinction between managing the portfolio on the one hand and delivering the programmes and projects on the other. Managing the portfolio is an ongoing business-as-usual function, comparable to financial management or control of risk within the organization. It is a permanent activity of the organization. Programmes and projects are temporary activities where the control and delivery standards used on the programmes and projects are those that are provided by the portfolio function.

At the corporate level, portfolio management provides an overview of the organization's total investment such that:

- Programmes and projects can be scrutinized and monitored to ensure ongoing alignment with the strategic objectives, and medium- and shorter-term goals
- The broad allocation of skilled programme and project resources can be optimized
- New requirements can be evaluated against current commitments
- Programme and project demands on the business-as-usual operations can be managed and coordinated at the corporate level
- The organization, via benefits analysis and realization at the portfolio level, will know what benefits and changes to expect.

1.1.1 Basic portfolio structure

Figure 1.1 shows the basic portfolio hierarchy of programmes and projects within a portfolio. This hierarchy allows for stand-alone projects that report directly at the portfolio level. This is not unexpected for key strategic projects.

1.2 WHY PORTFOLIO MANAGEMENT IS IMPORTANT

Most organizations operate in a complex environment with many programmes and projects going on at any one time. New programmes will be delivered in a complex, multi-project environment where there will be inevitable conflicts and interactions – such as competing priorities for scarce resources and interdependencies between projects. The question is: 'Can everything be done?' The portfolio function will be responsible for advising senior management (e.g. the Portfolio Board or management board – see section 4.3, Organization) on the portfolio, its progress against plans and any problems with conflicting priorities. The management team may have to make hard

Figure 1.1 Portfolio, programme and project hierarchy

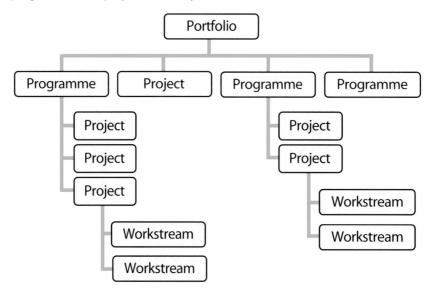

choices about programmes, projects and resources in the light of changing strategic direction and changing priorities:

- Programmes and projects – continue, complete, defer, stop
- Resources – deploy or redeploy; acquire; develop or remove.

Portfolio management provides the means to:

- Establish a structure for selecting the right programmes and projects
- Assess whether requirements can be accommodated within existing organizational capability and capacity
- Support programme and projects with unified standards, governance, frameworks and control
- Allocate the right resources to the right programmes and projects
- Ensure ongoing alignment of programmes and projects with strategic objectives and targets
- Resolve conflicts and contentions for scarce and costly resources

- Identify and manage interdependencies between programmes and projects
- Assess the true implications of the aggregate level of programme and project risk
- Monitor progress on programmes and projects against outcomes
- Ensure ongoing successful delivery of programmes and projects
- Optimize organizational investment
- Maximize returns from investment
- Achieve value-for-money savings and efficiency gains from programme and project rationalization.

1.3 WHAT DOES PORTFOLIO MANAGEMENT INVOLVE

Portfolio management involves establishing and maintaining an integrated process which links strategic objectives with the delivery of those objectives via programmes and projects (see Figure 1.2).

Figure 1.2 Strategic objectives with the delivery of those objectives via programmes and projects

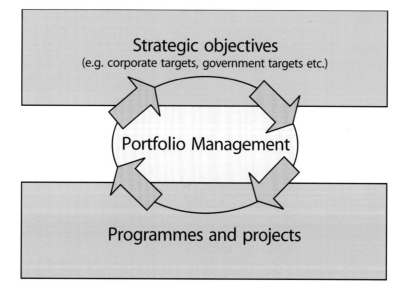

Strategic objectives
(e.g. corporate targets, government targets etc.)

Portfolio Management

Programmes and projects

1.4 BENEFITS OF PORTFOLIO MANAGEMENT

The portfolio management process involves collecting in one place pertinent (consistent) information about all the programmes and projects in an organization, and relating that information to the business requirements and capabilities of the organization. The outputs of the portfolio management will be informed decisions about:

- Choice of programme and projects
- Assignment of priorities
- Resource allocation
- Interdependencies
- Staffing and skills requirements and deployment
- Risks and benefits
- Gaps and overlaps in the portfolio

Figure 1.3 outlines this process in more detail.

1.5 STARTING PORTFOLIO MANAGEMENT

Whilst the benefits of portfolio management are considerable, for the adoption to work takes a considerable commitment, and there needs to be certain things in place for the adoption to work. These prerequisites include:

- Defining/agreeing the overall leadership
- Handling the complex cultural issues often associated with large (international?) portfolios

Figure 1.3 Managing portfolios of change (with MSP for programmes and PRINCE2 for projects)

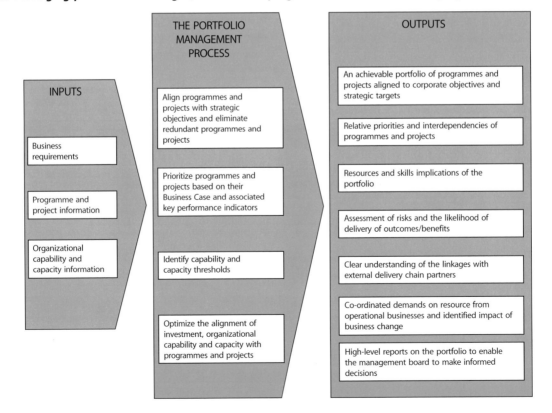

- Organizational capability in programme and project management with consistent standards applied to projects, and consistent standards applied to programmes
- Top management commitment to, and understanding of, the value of portfolio management
- Organization willingness to implement new processes to support and enable effective portfolio management.

NB – If the organization is already doing business planning, portfolio management should support the business planning process, and portfolio management should not require a considerable commitment to implement.

1.6 CHALLENGES

There are challenges that occur and need to be overcome when establishing portfolio management:

- Agreeing criteria for identifying programmes and projects within the organization, and distinguishing them for business-as-usual and operational activities/services
- Ensuring the portfolio process is integrated with the other business-as-usual processes for the successful implementation of portfolio management (e.g. HR, procurement, finance, quality etc.)
- Overcoming probable resistance from programmes and project teams to adopting common approaches to, for example, reporting progress and business case construction
- Countering the protests of business managers who do not want to see their projects possibly shifted to a lower priority

- Making sure that existing or new projects do not become hidden outside portfolio control or designated as business-as-usual (and therefore not needing to be reported within the portfolio)
- Ensuring in-flight programmes and projects are treated with the same consistency as new ones (if in-flight programmes and projects are allowed to continue with their own processes, the benefits of portfolio management are unlikely to be fully achieved)
- Making and following through on difficult decisions affecting the portfolio as a whole when resources are in short supply and timescales are tight
- Difficulty in allocating skilled resource due to structural, geographic and HR issues.

1.7 PROGRAMME AND PROJECT MANAGEMENT CAPABILITY

The organization will need the following best practice to be in place:

- Project management – using an approach such as PRINCE2, where the project objectives are clearly understood and agreed, roles and responsibilities are clear, and the deliverables, budgets and timeframes have been confirmed
- Programme management – using an approach such as MSP (Managing Successful Programmes), where related projects are coordinated and delivered as a business change.

Additionally, organizations should not attempt to establish a portfolio management function until they are confident that they have reached an appropriate level of maturity in their programme and project management approaches. The minimum recommended level is Level 3 of the OGC's P3M3 (Portfolio, Programme and Project Management Maturity Model), which helps organizations to assess their current capability in delivery. The P3M3 describes the

Table 1.1 Level 3 P3M3

Maturity	Project	Programme	Portfolio
Level 3 – *defined process*	The organization has its own centrally controlled project processes, **and** individual projects can flex within these processes to suit the particular project	The organization has its own centrally controlled programme processes **and** individual programmes can flex within these processes to suit the particular programme	The organization has its own centrally controlled programme and project processes. Individual programmes and projects can flex within these processes to suit particular programmes and/or projects. The organization also has its own portfolio management process

There is an overview of P3M3 in Annex B.

portfolio-, programme- and project-related activities within process areas that contribute to achieving a successful delivery outcome. Level 3 is shown in Table 1.1.

1.8 NO ONE CORRECT PORTFOLIO MANAGEMENT MODEL

Portfolio management may take place at many different levels within the organization – for example at the corporate level (the primary focus of this guidance), at the director level, within business units, and within the programmes and projects themselves.

Portfolio management may be enacted in very different ways:

- One organization may take a very hierarchical, top-down, corporate, model-driven approach (corporate portfolio _ directorate portfolios _ business unit portfolios _ programmes _ projects).
  - Choosing such a portfolio management model would probably imply a high degree of portfolio autonomy within directorates with few cross-directorate programmes or projects (and comparatively few cross-directorate dependencies and shared resources).

- Another organization may take an approach with themed portfolios in the corporate-level portfolio, using a more centrally driven approach (corporate portfolio _ themed portfolios _ programmes _ projects).
  - For example, all the web-related initiatives may be grouped into a web portfolio (to leverage critical web skills and resources), although these initiatives may be quite unrelated in terms of the areas of the organization they affect, and the business resources they will consume. All the regulatory-driven initiatives may be grouped in another portfolio (to leverage critical regulatory skills and resources). Again, these initiatives may be quite unrelated in terms of the areas of the organization they affect, and the business resources they will consume.
  - Choosing such a portfolio management model would probably imply a high degree of centralization and leverage of common/scarce resources across the organization with the corporate portfolio having a high degree of autonomy over directorates, with many cross-directorate programmes or projects (and a high number of cross-directorate dependencies and shared resources).

Effective portfolio management should also allow different views of the portfolio. For example, although the portfolio in the second example above may be organized in a centrally driven approach, the directorates or business units should be able to define the portfolio view that allows them to manage the commitments, ownerships and expected benefits that the corporate portfolio will expect of them.

It is important to recognize that one-size-fits-all is not the ideal approach to successful portfolio management. Different organizations have very different governance structures and arrangements for reporting on progress. The critical factor for success is to identify the corporate governance structures – e.g. a large federal organization with completely autonomous business units contrasted with a small organization for tighter central control, or a department with complex arms-length relationships with non-departmental bodies – that will work for that organization. The governance structures for portfolio management must be mapped on to the organization's relational structures.

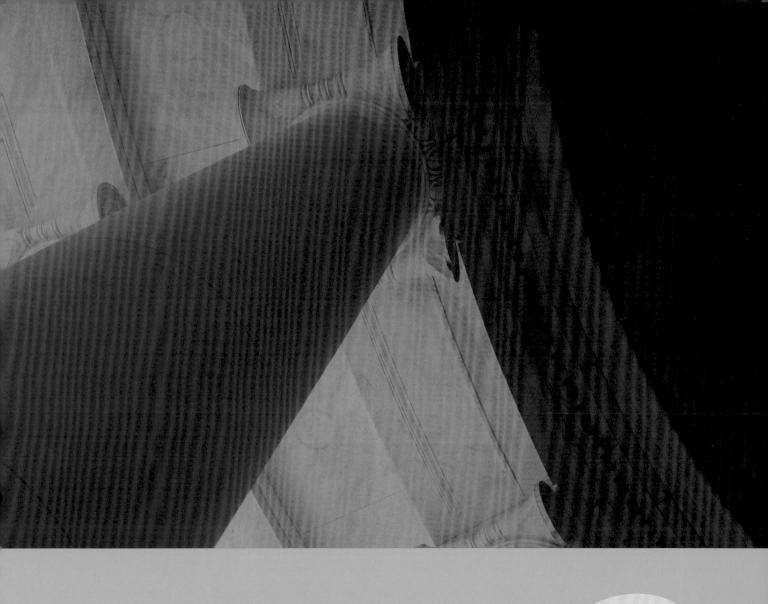

Portfolio
management
principles

2

2 Portfolio management principles

The creation and management of the portfolio should be underpinned by reference to principles of portfolio management that are:

- Universal – they apply to every portfolio
- Self-validating – they have been proven in practice
- Empowering – they give practitioners the ability to successfully shape and manage ongoing corporate change comprised of multiple programmes and projects;

and acknowledge the need for

- A clear governance structure within the organization that ensures projects are evaluated, prioritized and approved based on business goals and objectives
- A project and programme planning, development and management approach that involves all main stakeholders early on, and to the greatest extent possible
- Managing the projects and programmes in the organization as a portfolio so that scarce resources can be directed toward those projects that deliver the most value and flexibility can be assured when priorities may shift during the course of any project.

Often in a problem programme or project, the goal itself is seldom the problem. More often projects don't deliver the desired result, or fail altogether because of inadequate governance, poor project management or failure to direct scarce resources in the most productive way.
Organizations that develop and deploy clear governance, project/programme management disciplines and effective portfolio management will realize much greater value from their change initiatives and investments.

If the following principles are observed the portfolio will be more likely to consistently deliver value for money, with control, visibility and the right balance for the organization. These principles (see Figure 2.1) are:

- Remain aligned with corporate strategy
- Have a balanced portfolio
- Projects and programmes are owned investments
- See one organization-wide picture
- Ensure repeatability and control
- Keep learning and evolving.

2.1 REMAIN ALIGNED WITH CORPORATE STRATEGY

A portfolio is a corporate (or business-as-usual) activity that prioritizes and manages programmes and projects of change to deliver value to the organization. Whilst programmes and projects may come into and go out of the corporate portfolio, the corporate portfolio remains. The portfolio is made up of a changing roster of programmes (and the projects that comprise them) and stand-alone projects.

These programmes and stand-alone projects may have no direct relationship with each other. However, within the portfolio all programmes and projects contribute to delivering the strategy of the organization.

The portfolio (via its programmes and projects) often has to prove or disprove strategic ideas. Because of this, and the need to possibly rebalance the portfolio, there has to be effective feedback from the programmes and projects (via the portfolio) to the strategists and leaders of the organization. Also, as external drivers may cause possibly frequent changes of strategic direction, the portfolio must be adaptable enough to keep pace with these.

Figure 2.1 Portfolio management principles

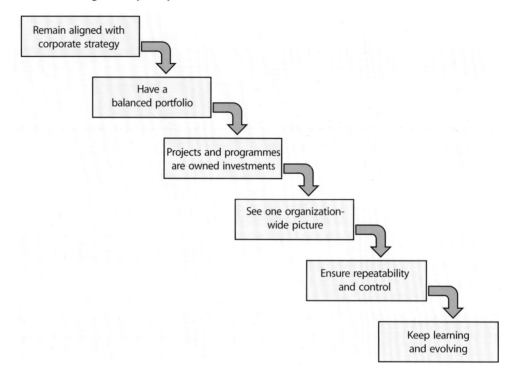

The portfolio must ensure the strategic drivers are extended downwards, via visibility, governance and control, into the programmes, projects and business change activities. The portfolio must not allow programmes and projects to become detached from, or misaligned with, corporate strategy.

2.2 HAVE A BALANCED PORTFOLIO

Each organization will have its own appetite and need for change. The sum of these will be expressed in the nature and balance of the corporate portfolio for that organization. As the balance of strategic drivers for the organization changes, so should the nature and balance of the portfolio. This balance should extend to the number of programmes and projects in the portfolio being

manageable, and avoiding complexity when segmenting the portfolio (two common problems in portfolio design).

Whilst there are many profile aspects of portfolio balance to consider [e.g. spend and return, risk, delivery against short-, medium- and longer-term targets, agreed resource usage, acceptable business impact (likely to be most pronounced at transition etc.)], the fundamental question 'Will this portfolio deliver against the organization's strategy, in its current context?' should be asked.

2.3 PROJECTS AND PROGRAMMES ARE OWNED INVESTMENTS

Programmes, the projects that comprise them and any stand-alone projects in the portfolio must be business owned. This means that programmes must have named Senior Responsible Owners (MSP terminology; may also be known as 'programme sponsor/owner/executive') and projects must have Project Executives (PRINCE2 terminology; may also be known as 'project sponsor/owner') that are accountable for their programmes and/or projects. In some organizations this is extending to the delivery of the projects and programmes and realization of benefits being explicitly in the performance contracts of the individuals in the Senior Responsible Owner and Project Executives roles, and is forming part of annual appraisal, earning a bonus etc. In a programme environment the ownership and accountability of the Senior Responsible Owner will take precedence over that of the Project Executives of the projects in the programme.

Portfolio management means running programmes and projects as investments, with costs, expected benefits and timescales for the costs and realization of benefits. In this model each programme and project will need its own business case. A key element of portfolio review is assessing the actual and expected delivery of benefits (and any enablers for these benefits) against the original and latest sanctioned versions of the business cases. It is important to retain visibility of the commitment made in the original sanctioned business cases as the nature and aggregate of the disparities between these and the latest sanctioned business cases give valuable information about the nature and quality of capabilities, such as planning and estimating, that will be core to the performance of the portfolio.

There is a simple test for the validity of a programme. A programme usually adds cost over the aggregate of the costs of the projects in the programme. This overhead is only justified by the added value in managing the complexity (dependencies, risks, issues, resources, delivery of benefits etc.) across the projects at a lower cost than if done by the projects themselves. If the programme level costs cannot be justified by their added value, there may not be a genuine programme.

2.4   SEE ONE ORGANIZATION-WIDE PICTURE

For this to work, there will need to be standardization of information, categorization and presentation both vertically (from the portfolio down to programmes and projects) and horizontally (across programmes and across projects).

Where possible the portfolio should look for single, unitary sources of information. For example, who will own and provide programme and project financial information to the portfolio? Will it be the programmes and projects or the finance function? Whose financial information will have primacy? These are the types of question that will need to be answered. As portfolio management is a corporate-level activity, adopting and setting corporate standards and processes will be necessary if it is to work. Within this, there are three sub-principles:

■ Where they exist, the portfolio should ideally look to use the organization's existing governance and control frameworks as these should provide the necessary structures and visibility. This alignment should extend to (in terms of expression, unit of value, nature of analysis and minimum frequency of reporting) the corporate controls used in, for example:
- finance and accounting
- human resource management
- risk and issue management
- quality systems
- operations and performance
- information technology
- customer and stakeholder satisfaction
- sourcing and procurement
- contract management
- legislative compliance
- information management.

- In a dispute, as the existing control standard will normally prevail (this is particularly true with the finance and risk functions), the portfolio should look to adopt the existing control standard, and do any tailoring within the portfolio environment.
- Should a control standard exist but be inadequate, the portfolio should look to augment, not replace, the control standard and, if necessary, do this within the portfolio environment.

2.5   ENSURE REPEATABILITY AND CONTROL

The portfolio, programme and project processes should be standardized and repeatable, with consistent management products (e.g. templates and nature of Programme Business Cases, Project Briefs etc.) and specialist products (e.g. Technology Impact Assessment) across the programmes and projects that comprise the portfolio. Additionally, the data and information collected and used by the portfolio should comply with Principle 4. Without this level of consistency across process, product and data, the portfolio will not have the ability to compare either across projects at a point in time, or across projects across time. If there is not consistency at the project level, there cannot be comparability at the programme level, or understanding at the portfolio level.

2.6   KEEP LEARNING AND EVOLVING

A portfolio is an evolving organization that should reflect on and improve its own performance over its evolution. This means that the portfolio should look to both:

- Formally assess its performance, and
- Innovate to improve its performance

The assessing of portfolio performance might include a number of different measures, such as aggregate ROI, individual financial performance of projects, number of projects within their business case tolerances etc.

Innovation might include providing earlier support to projects that may go off track and looking for experienced and successful Senior Responsible Owners and Project Executives to formally mentor those who are new to the role.

Good portfolio governance also requires approaches to adjusting and adapting the controls and performance measures on the basis of experience and results so far and future expectations. This is explored later in Section 4, 'Portfolio governance'. Portfolios perform better, and reach superior performance earlier, where members of the portfolio team (and the programme and project management) accept that they are part of a learning and evolving organization. Such a reflective stance may require certain adjustments to be built into the governance of the portfolio. Typically this may be done with a formal process of portfolio health-check (where the portfolio is health-checked, and not just the programmes and projects within it). This allows the portfolio team and the individuals within it to better formalize and structure their learning as the portfolio progresses.

2.7   THE NEXT SECTIONS

2.7.1   Section 3 – Portfolio process

This section identifies the how the portfolio is defined and then managed, and takes a process-based view, answering the question, 'What do you do in what order?'

Main headings:

- Overview
- Defining the Portfolio Strategy
- Creating the first version of the Portfolio Schedule and Portfolio Plan
- Categorizing the portfolio
- Prioritizing the portfolio
- Segmenting the portfolio

- Confirm the Portfolio Strategy, Portfolio Schedule and Portfolio Plan
- Tracking and action
- Review and reprioritization.

2.7.2 Section 4 – Portfolio governance

This section identifies and discusses those themes that comprise the governance of the portfolio. It includes areas of MSP (i.e. the Governance Themes) and PRINCE2 (i.e. the Components) that are relevant to ensuring the appropriate governance of the portfolio, and also how they fit into and support that theme of portfolio governance.

Main headings:

- Overview
- Portfolio management approach
- Organization
- Integrated programme and project management
- Stakeholder Engagement and Leadership
- Benefits realization
- Portfolio planning and control
- Risk management.

2.7.3 Reading the next sections

The reader may read Section 3 straight away to understand the process of how the portfolio is defined and then managed. Alternatively the reader could look at the different governance themes in Section 4. I would recommend the reader look at the Section 4 themes 'Portfolio management approach', 'Organization' and 'Integrated programme and project management', before tackling Section 3.

Portfolio process

3 Portfolio process

3.1 OVERVIEW

This section takes a process-based view, answering the question 'What do you do in what order?' to define and then manage the portfolio.

3.1.1 Portfolio steps and phases

The eight process steps fall into three main phases as shown in Table 3.1.

Table 3.1 Portfolio steps and phases

Steps in the Portfolio Process	Major portfolio phases
1 Defining the Portfolio Strategy	**Inception (Steps 1–2)**
2 Creating the first version of the Portfolio Schedule and Portfolio Plan	■ States the expected scope of the portfolio for the defined planning period (Portfolio Strategy)
	■ Lists the programmes and projects that will deliver this (Portfolio Schedule)
	■ Shows how the delivery will happen (Portfolio Plan)
3 Categorizing the portfolio	**Definition (Steps 3–6)**
4 Prioritizing the portfolio	■ Gives the views of the portfolio that will be used for assessing performance (categorizing)
5 Segmenting the portfolio	■ States which programmes and projects will have priority for resources in delivering against the Portfolio Strategy (prioritizing)
6 Confirm the Portfolio Strategy, Portfolio Schedule and Portfolio Plan	■ Sets out the organizational ownership for the programmes and projects of the portfolio (segmenting)
	■ Restates the scope, content and delivery plan for the portfolio, with its governance and control (confirm)
7 Tracking and action	**Delivery (Steps 7–8)**
8 Portfolio review and reprioritization	■ Monitor the performance of the programmes and projects, taking corrective action as needed (tracking)
	■ Monitor the performance of the portfolio, taking corrective action as needed via programme/project reprioritization and adjustment to the Portfolio Strategy (portfolio review)

3.1.2 Outline of the process steps

Step 1 – Defining the Portfolio Strategy

- Alignment with corporate objectives (with some form of rating or scoring for the programmes and projects to be in the portfolio)
- Ensuring balance of deliverability and ambition in the portfolio
- Setting priorities when competing for scarce capacity.

Step 2 – Creating the first version of the Portfolio Schedule and Portfolio Plan

- The first version of the Portfolio Schedule lists the programmes and projects expected to deliver against the Portfolio Strategy
- Assessing current projects – to what extent the individual and aggregation of current projects will deliver against the Portfolio Strategy
- Generating the other programmes and projects – the portfolio gap is filled by listing, scheduling and then incepting the programmes and projects that will fill the portfolio gaps
- The first version of the Portfolio Plan details how the portfolio is to be delivered.

Step 3 – Categorizing the portfolio

- Segments the programmes and projects into categories
- Allow the portfolio to be viewed from a number of perspectives.

Step 4 – Prioritizing the portfolio

- Within each category, and across the categories, the programmes and projects in the created portfolio must be prioritized

- Priority of the programmes and projects within the portfolio to be aligned to the organization's strategy reflected in the milestones of the Portfolio Strategy.

Step 5 – Segmenting the portfolio

- Ensuring the right business ownership and commitment within, and supported by, the right programme and project governance
- Focus in this step is not the balance and nature of the individual programmes and projects, but rather a cut of the Portfolio Organization
- Confirm structure and other governance to be able to own and deliver against the Portfolio Strategy.

Step 6 – Confirm the Portfolio Strategy, Portfolio Schedule and Portfolio Plan

- Agreed triangulation across the Portfolio Strategy, Portfolio Schedule and Portfolio Plan
- The right balance of strategic alignment, deliverability, risk and resource consumption
- The three signed off/accepted by the Portfolio Board, under advice from the Portfolio Director.

Step 7 – Tracking and action

- How the delivery of the programmes and projects in the portfolio will be monitored to ensure they are on track relative to their business cases, delivery plans and resource utilization plans
- Not looking at the performance of the portfolio as a whole, but very much at the performance of the individual programmes and projects in the portfolio
- Being able to compare performance across the programmes and projects will depend on standardized processes of programme and project definition, planning and reporting.

Step 8 – Review and reprioritization

- How the portfolio as a whole will be reviewed to ensure it is, and will, deliver against the Portfolio Strategy and the Portfolio Plan
- How the Portfolio Strategy is to be reviewed to ensure that the portfolio remains aligned to the (possibly fast-changing) strategy of the organization.

3.1.3 Cycles of and within the portfolio steps

The eight steps in the portfolio process have clear cycles between and within themselves. These are discussed later and shown in Figure 3.1.

3.2 PROCESS STEP 1 – DEFINING THE PORTFOLIO STRATEGY

A portfolio is created to allow the prioritized delivery of change (programmes and projects) to achieve the strategic goals of the organization, within the constraints of that organization in its context (e.g. human and financial resources, risk appetite, regulation). For the portfolio to deliver it must therefore have the strategic goals of the organization and its contextual parameters as its terms of reference.

This translation of the organization's strategy, goals and targets into change initiatives is done by creating and validating the Portfolio Strategy.

Figure 3.1 Cycles of the portfolio steps

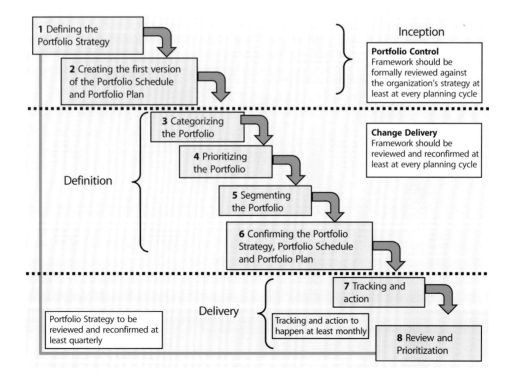

The Portfolio Strategy includes:

- The rules of the process by which the portfolio is built (including the rules of programme and project selection, prioritization, categorization, segmentation etc.)
- The parameters within which the portfolio will be managed (e.g. risk, financial, resource)
- Expected outcomes of change initiatives aligned to the strategic goals and targets of the organization and its business units
- A timeline of how the strategic goals and targets will be met over time (i.e. achievement/milestone dates and review points)

The Portfolio Strategy sets the terms, organizational scope and parameters for the definition and delivery of the portfolio. The Portfolio Strategy is part of a triumvirate that also includes the Portfolio Schedule and Portfolio Plan. Confirming the balance and cohesiveness of the final versions of the Portfolio Strategy, Portfolio Schedule and Portfolio Plan will take a number of iterations.

As the iterations are worked through, it is important to ensure that the Portfolio Strategy, Portfolio Schedule and Portfolio Plan remain synchronized and cross-reinforcing. The process for defining the first version of the Portfolio Strategy is shown below.

3.2.1 Define organizational/group level and functional change goals

The portfolio function will need to see and understand the organization's vision and mission, and also the organization's strategy and objectives. From the defined organizational- or group-level objectives and targets, it should be possible to list those changes that will be delivered at the organizational/group level. The defined organizational/group-level objectives and targets should include any targets for functional changes and improvements (e.g. for HR, finance etc.). From these,

functional area changes, that may have a group-wide impact, and may be delivered at the organizational/group level, should be listed.

This gives the corporate-level elements of the Portfolio Strategy. This should include the financial and performance parameters of the organization's portfolio for that year (e.g. spend parameters for the year, performance targets to be achieved by change initiatives across the organization) as well as that part of the organization's portfolio that will be delivered at the highest level (i.e. by change initiatives that will be managed at the organizational/group level – the corporate-level change initiatives) and by/for the functions of the organization.

From this it should be possible to create first versions of delivery and achievement milestones for the organization's overall portfolio, the corporate-level change initiatives and also for the functional change initiatives for that year (reflecting the relative priority and importance of the organization's objectives for that year), with indicative spend for these.

3.2.2 Define business-unit-level change goals

There is still the need to cascade: understand the performance targets at the operational and business unit (BU) level, and agree the change targets that will then need to be delivered by the change initiatives for and/or by that BU.

In the operations of the organization, the corporate strategy and objectives (for that year) are translated into high-level operational plans that are owned by the BUs. For the BUs to deliver against these, they will need to define programmes and projects of change. Before the right mix of programmes and projects can be designed, the delivery targets of the programmes and projects must the set.

The output of this activity should be the first version of delivery and achievement milestones for the BU-level portion of the organization's overall portfolio (reflecting the relative priority and importance of the objectives agreed for the BUs for that year) with indicative spend for these.

The Portfolio Director will need to accept/reject these first versions of proposals, bringing to bear their understanding of the organizational and change capabilities, in-flight change initiatives, and risk appetite and resource constraints. For this reason, the portfolio function, and in particular the Portfolio Director, will need to be comfortable with how the strategic inputs cascade down into operational and BU-level performance parameters.

In understanding the organizational/group-level, functional- and BU-level change goals, and translating these into portfolio goals it is important that portfolio goal generation is a function and outcome of the corporate goal generation process. It is imperative that the portfolio does not independently generate its own goals, otherwise there will be both duplication of effort and a lack of combined aligned objectives.

3.2.3 Confirm the rules of prioritization, categorization and segmentation

The first version of the Portfolio Strategy should now contain:

- Expected outcomes of change initiatives aligned to the strategic goals and targets of the organization, and its business units
- A schedule of how the strategic goals and targets will be met over time (i.e. quantified achievement milestones with dates and review points).

This information should be used to inform and confirm the processes and standards by which the portfolio is built, including the rules and content of programme and project selection and management. This is discussed below.

- **Prioritization** – the rules of the prioritization of programmes and projects; must be seen to be aligned to the organization's strategy and goals. The application of the rules and the ensuing priority of the programmes and projects within the portfolio will be reflected in, and congruent with, the milestones of the first version of the Portfolio Strategy.
- **Categorization** – the rules of how to segment the programmes and projects into different themes, which allows them to be viewed and managed from a number of (ideally strategically defined) perspectives. This must cover how this is to be done (i.e. the principles of categorization), together with any mandatory views or categories that must be applied to the portfolio. The outcome should be the categories that provide the views that the organization needs to be able to assess partial (i.e. by view) and aggregate delivery against the first version of the Portfolio Strategy.
- **Segmentation** – the rules and principles of how the Portfolio Organization (structure and other governance) is to be achieved. This is the rule set that gives the right ownership of programmes and projects, allowing delivery against the first version of the Portfolio Strategy.

3.3 PROCESS STEP 2 – CREATING THE FIRST VERSION OF THE PORTFOLIO SCHEDULE AND PORTFOLIO PLAN

Setting and agreeing the first version of the Portfolio Strategy is the foundation for building the Portfolio Schedule and the Portfolio Plan. The Portfolio Strategy,

Portfolio Plan and Portfolio Schedule form a triangulation confirming:

- Ongoing alignment of the portfolio with corporate objectives and goals (Portfolio Strategy)
- Detailed, owned programmes and projects operating within defined control and constraints (Portfolio Schedule)
- Clear strategic delivery, spend and benefit realization milestones (Portfolio Plan).

To be able to build the first version of the Portfolio Schedule and Portfolio Plan, the first version of the Portfolio Strategy should contain:

- The rules of the process by which the portfolio is built (including the rules of programme and project selection, prioritization, categorization, segmentation etc.)
- A timeline of the expected outcomes of change initiatives at the corporate level, aligned to the strategic goals and targets of the organization
- The parameters within which the corporate portfolio will be managed (e.g. risk, financial, resource etc.)
- Timelines of the expected outcomes of change initiatives at the BU level and also for the functions, aligned to the strategic goals and targets of the BUs and functions
- A first version of the parameters (e.g. the risk, financial, resource etc. limits) within/for which the changes for that part of the organization (i.e. BUs and functions) will be managed and delivered.

These have to be agreed as deliverable by the relevant, owning part of the organization and the portfolio function/Portfolio Director.

The first version of the Portfolio Schedule and first version of the Portfolio Plan should complement these with:

- First version of the Portfolio Schedule – the programmes and projects of the overall corporate portfolio and any sub-portfolios (e.g. group level, functional or BU) that will allow delivery against the first version of the Portfolio Strategy, with the (draft) attributes of each programme or project
- First version of the Portfolio Plan – how the projects and programmes of the first version of the Portfolio Schedule will deliver against the first version of the Portfolio Strategy, with a focus on the timing of incurring cost and delivering benefits.

3.3.1 Creating the first version of the Portfolio Schedule

The first version of the Portfolio Strategy provides the target and parameters for defining and agreeing the nature and composition of the overall corporate portfolio and any sub-portfolios (e.g. group level, functional or BU). The first version of the Portfolio Strategy can be taken forward, as it has been built, reviewed and agreed as:

- Meeting the strategic need
- Delivering against the goals and targets
- Achievable

within the defined parameters of cost, risk, resource and commitments around the in-flight change initiatives.

With these clear goals, the programmes and projects that will deliver against the Portfolio Strategy may be defined. As the programmes and projects are designed, there are core attributes that must be listed (or at least drafted) for each programme or project. These will include:

- Programme/project name
- High-level statement of what the programme/project will deliver
- Which parts of the organization the programme/project will impact
- Expected costs
- Delivery timelines (i.e. what, when)

- Segmentation of the programme/project (i.e. in which portfolio/sub-portfolio/programme; confirming the part of the organization where the programme/project will be owned)
- Owner of the programme/project
- Categorization of the programme/project
- Priority of the programme/project.

(NB – For greater detail of the core attributes of a programme refer to MSP, and for projects refer to PRINCE2.)

The first version of the Portfolio Schedule lists the programmes and projects that are to be delivered. It should also include proposed performance details relative to the following views of the portfolio (and any sub-portfolios):

- Categorization – the expected individual and aggregate performance of the projects that are grouped in different categories, e.g. infrastructure, regulatory, cost reduction
- Prioritization – the expected individual and aggregate performance of the projects that are grouped in the different tiers of prioritization. It may be appropriate to include truncation scenarios, e.g. if due to constraint, the bottom tier of projects, or a particular set of programmes/projects are not to be delivered, what impact does this have on:
  - Delivery against the Portfolio Strategy, and
  - The availability of released resource (e.g. money, particular skills) for use in other programmes/projects?
- Segmentation – the expected impact of owning and delivering their projects and programmes on the parts of the organization that must give up resource to ensure ownership and delivery. This should include those in formal roles (e.g. Senior Responsible Owner, senior user) and those who although not in formal roles are to contribute to the programme or project definition and delivery.

Assessing current projects

The first version of the Portfolio Schedule lists the programmes and projects that are to be delivered to meet the Portfolio Strategy. This step assesses to what extent the individual and aggregation of current projects will deliver against the Portfolio Strategy.

Although it may seem paradoxical, the first version of the Portfolio Schedule (with its list of desired projects) is created before the assessment of current projects for inclusion in the Portfolio Schedule. This is done for a very good reason. If it were accepted that the current projects would form the basis of the Portfolio Schedule, then it is highly likely that the Portfolio Schedule would not meet the expectations of the Portfolio Strategy. The Portfolio Schedule would quickly become stale, with an unchanging feel about it, and the Portfolio Strategy would need to be watered down to meet the delivery and scope implied by the existing projects. The argument for current projects forming the basis of the Portfolio Schedule, with new programmes and projects then being added, would be stronger for an organization that has little or no change to its strategic goals over successive planning cycles.

This step should result in a statement listing:

1. Those existing projects that should be carried forward unchanged to the Portfolio Schedule, listing what aspects of the first version of the Portfolio Strategy they deliver against
2. Those existing projects that should be carried forward to the Portfolio Schedule, but with modification, listing the modification/changes to the project (scope, goals, cost, benefits etc.) and what aspects of the first version of the Portfolio Strategy they would now deliver against
3. Those existing projects that should be stopped
4. Gaps in the Portfolio Schedule that will need to be filled by other projects for delivery against the Portfolio Strategy.

As with previous steps, if the organizational portfolio is composed of BU and functional portfolios there may well be some iteration before a clear and acceptable picture emerges. In this process the Portfolio Director and Portfolio Board may well need to give clear guidance and support in proposing or endorsing the cutting and amending of existing programmes and projects, as many people may feel very uncomfortable with this.

Generating the other programmes and projects

The portfolio gaps are filled by listing the programmes and projects that will fill out the Portfolio Schedule to deliver against the Portfolio Strategy. Although several programmes or projects may be listed and detailed, it is important to note that many of the newly listed programmes and projects will be scheduled for inception months later.

The new programmes and projects, like the existing projects and programmes that are taken forward into the portfolio, must be described to include the detail that is expected of the other programmes and projects in the portfolio.

Listing the new projects should not be overly onerous, as the first version of the Portfolio Schedule and first version of the Portfolio Plan will already have listed at high level the indicative programmes and projects that would deliver against the first version of the Portfolio Strategy. However, defining the scope of new projects and programmes to fill gaps in the portfolio may be difficult and challenging, and the scope of other projects/programmes will probably have to flex to make room whilst keeping their scope clear, managing common resources, stakeholders, maintaining governance etc.

3.3.2 Creating the first version of the Portfolio Plan

The first version of the Portfolio Strategy has provided the target and parameters for defining and agreeing the nature and composition of the overall corporate portfolio and any sub-portfolios (e.g. group level, functional or BU). The first version of the Portfolio Schedule has listed the expected programmes and projects with attributes of each programme or project. Creating the first version of the Portfolio Plan takes the aggregation of the draft programmes and projects from the first version of the Portfolio Schedule and, by considering their attributes in relation to the requirements of the Portfolio Strategy, defines a Portfolio Plan, with programme and project:

- Prioritization
- Categorization
- Segmentation
- Ownership
- Resource profiling
- Level of investment
- Benefits profiling

aligned to deliver against the first version of the Portfolio Strategy.

Although this is only the first version of the Portfolio Plan, it should still list:

- What organizational/business changes will be delivered, and into which part of the organization
- When the organizational/business changes will be delivered
- Which programme or project will deliver which organizational/business changes
- What resources will be used to deliver the changes
- Who will own, deliver and accept the changes
- The scale of (accepted) risk associated with delivering the changes.

In aligning possible programmes and projects against the first version of the Portfolio Strategy, the first version of the Portfolio Plan should address standard issues associated with the management of multiple programmes and projects, such as:

- Relative prioritization

- Possible duplication
- Resource scarcity and conflict
- Bottlenecks
- Dependencies
- Ensuring business ownership of the programmes and projects
- Countering the significant risks associated with business-as-usual diverting resources from the projects/programmes or having other adverse impacts
- Danger of change overload (too much change activity affecting the organization at any one time)
- Application of an effective risk management process to address any arising risks and issues.

Inevitably, in drafting the first versions of the Portfolio Strategy, Portfolio Schedule and Portfolio Plan, there will be a large amount of horse-trading and discussion, as the composition, ownership and priority of the organizational level and sub/functional-level portfolios are debated and refined.

The first versions of the Portfolio Strategy, Portfolio Schedule and Portfolio Plan must now be reviewed to:

- Clarify business ownership
- List the new and existing projects that will comprise the Portfolio Schedule and map against those listed in the first version of the Portfolio Schedule.
- Confirm the achievability relative to the level of risk (financial, operational, deliverability, reputational etc.).

3.3.3 Confirming the first version of the Portfolio Strategy, Portfolio Schedule and Portfolio Plan

The first versions of the Portfolio Strategy, Portfolio Schedule and Portfolio Plan outline what is to be delivered by the portfolio, and show how this is to be achieved. Once a triangulation has been achieved it should be

confirmed and signed off by the Portfolio Board. The signing off of the first versions of the Portfolio Strategy, Portfolio Schedule and Portfolio Plan marks a major step in confirming the portfolio that the organization will take forward.

In constructing its first versions of the Portfolio Strategy, Portfolio Schedule and Portfolio Plan, the organization has, in integrated and quantitative terms, defined its appetite for change, across dimensions and measures including:

- Ambition for change (the balance of transformational projects against non-transformational projects)
- Risk tolerance (the level of aggregate risk across the portfolio and the level of individual risk ascribed to the top tier projects)
- Tolerance for disruption (the numbers of people in defined programme and project roles, and those contributing to definition or delivery)
- Budget for change – for the portfolio, as well as the programmes and projects within it.

3.4 PROCESS STEP 3 – CATEGORIZING THE PORTFOLIO

There is now the task of digging deeper into the portfolio and testing the rules and impact of the categorization, prioritization and segmentation. This is to ensure deliverability, confirm alignment against the Portfolio Strategy and resolve conflicts and constraints that the first versions of the Portfolio Strategy, Portfolio Schedule and Portfolio Plan may raise.

The first task is to review the categories that were created for viewing the programmes and projects against defined strategic drivers for the first version of the Portfolio Schedule. The created views (allowing the portfolio to be assessed from a number of perspectives) must be tested.

This step must confirm that the:

- Programmes and projects fit with their designated categories
- Categories are consistent without any ill-fitting programmes or projects
- Defined categories give the desired views
- Attributes of the categories give the wanted visibility of the performance of that category
- New categories are not needed
- No programme or project needs to be moved to another category.

If the above points cannot be confirmed, the categorizing must be reviewed and re-cut until the Portfolio Board is satisfied with the nature, balance, visibility and control that the categorization brings to the portfolio. The categorization must have the full set of programmes and projects listed in the created portfolio assigned to the defined categories.

3.4.1 Tiered categorization

There are several techniques available for categorizing programmes and projects. For example, projects can be categorized according to the role of the development in the organization's business. Table 3.2 suggests one broad such categorization, taken from the OGC Portfolio Management Guide.

Another more IT-focused categorization model is the Gartner Segmentation Model in Table 3.3, taken from *Setting Accurate IT Investment Levels Demands an Appropriate Framework* (Gartner White Papers).

Table 3.3 Gartner tiered categorization

Infrastructure
Mandated by law
Mandated by IT principles
Non-strategic
Strategic

3.4.2 Two-dimension categorization

Another approach to categorization of projects is the two-dimensional categorization, plotting high to low scores for two attributes or dimensions of the proposed

Table 3.2 OGC tiered categorization

Mandatory	Required to satisfy a statutory or legal requirement. A non-discretionary development
Business support	Required to support the automation or development of business procedures in core business areas and business support functions
Strategic	Developments essential to the long-term future well-being of the organization
Experimental	Developments which may lead to beneficial facilities in the longer term, and which require initial investment for investigation, pilots etc.
Infrastructure	Developments and investments which underpin business-specific developments, but are not targeted at a single application or business area. They may produce no direct benefits in themselves
Maintenance	Developments required to ensure the continuing smooth operation of existing systems, services and facilities, including technology refreshment
Inter-organizational	Developments which enable the organization to communicate and share resources (including data) with other organizations

programme/projects. Figure 3.2 is the pain vs. gain chart. This assesses proposed developments in terms of the:

- Ease of implementation (pain), against
- Impact on the business (gain).

The resulting matrix is shown in Figure 3.2, with suggestions for the decision on implementation of the proposed development.

The two-dimensional pain vs. gain chart is often used as a prioritization tool, and of course the tiered and two-dimensional model may be used in tandem to achieve prioritization within categorization. Prioritization is discussed further below.

3.5 PROCESS STEP 4 – PRIORITIZING THE PORTFOLIO

Within each category, and across the categories, the programmes and projects in the portfolio must be

prioritized. The nature of the prioritization must be seen to be aligned to the organization's strategy and goals.

It is likely that the demands of the Portfolio Strategy mean that the initial portfolio prioritization should be reviewed and tested, to confirm the cost/delivery profile of the programmes and projects within the portfolio reflect the performance milestones of the Portfolio Strategy. The prioritization of the portfolio must therefore be seen to be supporting delivery against the Portfolio Strategy, and enabling the Portfolio Plan. It is important to ensure that stakeholders remain focused on achieving the organization's outcomes when undertaking the prioritization.

3.5.1 Tiered prioritization

All the programmes and projects in the organization's portfolio should be grouped according to the organization's tiered prioritization model. The OGC's prioritization levels are shown in Table 3.4 and tiered for both the public and private sector.

Figure 3.2 Two-dimensional categorization

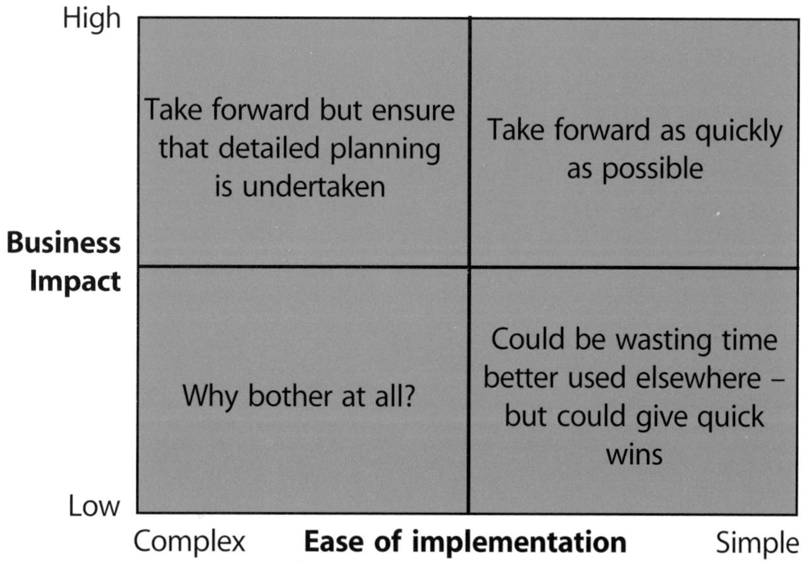

Table 3.4 OGC tiered prioritization

Mission critical	Public sector:
	Projects are essential to the successful delivery of a major legislative requirement, a major policy initiative announced and owned by a government minister. They are also mission critical if, in the event of project failure, there are catastrophic implications for delivery of a public service, national security or the internal operation of a public sector operation.
	Private sector:
	Projects are essential to the successful delivery of corporate strategy and are owned by a board member. They are also critical such that in the event of project failure, there are catastrophic implications for customer service or service delivery.
Highly desirable	Public sector:
	Projects are important (but not essential) for major initiatives as above; or they are essential to the successful delivery of a minor legislative requirement, a high profile (but not PSA) target or other government policy initiatives. Alternatively, if they fail, there are serious (but not catastrophic) implications for major initiatives and/or catastrophic implications for the delivery of non-key public services or the realization of significant business benefits.
	Private sector:
	Projects are important (but not essential) for performance improvement or are essential to the successful delivery of non-essential changes. If the project fails, there may be serious implications for major initiatives and adverse implications for the delivery of non-critical support services.
Desirable	Public and private sectors:
	Programmes or projects are all those that do not meet the mission critical or highly desirable criteria.

3.5.2 Two-dimensional prioritization

Two-dimensional categorization can also be used for prioritization, with the output groupings being the tiers of prioritization. The tiers below are as per the two-dimensional categorization in Figure 3.2:

- Take forward as quickly as possible (high business impact and high ease of implementation)
- Take forward but ensure that detailed planning is undertaken (high business impact and low ease of implementation)

- Could be wasting time better used elsewhere – but could give quick wins (low business impact and high ease of implementation)
- Why bother at all? (low business impact and low ease of implementation).

3.6 PROCESS STEP 5 – SEGMENTING THE PORTFOLIO

This step is very much about ensuring the right business ownership and commitment within, and supported by, the right programme and project governance and ensuring that programmes and projects have appropriate levels of governance in place. With a top-down process of generating a portfolio to meet the strategic change needs of the organization, there is a risk that the high-level expectations (as set out in the Portfolio Strategy) cannot be met by the operational areas without change overload.

With the first version of the Portfolio Strategy, Portfolio Schedule and Portfolio Plan defined, there will be a need to dig more deeply into the Portfolio Schedule and Portfolio Plan to confirm that the programmes and projects listed in the Portfolio Schedule and Portfolio Plan will be owned by the right part of the organization, and that part of the organization will commit the resources implicit in the Portfolio Schedule and Portfolio Plan.

It is important to note that the focus in this step is not the balance and nature of the individual programmes and projects, but rather a cut of the Portfolio Organization, structure and other governance to be able to own and deliver against the Portfolio Strategy.

The first version of the Portfolio Schedule and Portfolio Plan will have listed the programmes and projects that are to be delivered to support the Portfolio Strategy. The segmentation and ownership step acts as a confirmation, making sure that the programmes and projects have the necessary ownership, commitment, controls and visibility to deliver against the Portfolio Strategy. This may result in changes to the structure, governance (e.g. organization) or control of the portfolio. The outcome of this step should be a redrafting of the Portfolio Organization (the portfolio hierarchy going down to the level of the projects).

The Portfolio Organization should now show, for each programme and project, the

- BU/functional area that owns the programme/project
- Individual who will be the Senior Responsible Owner/Project Executive

- Business Change Manager/Change Manager
- People who will need to be on the Programme Boards and Project Boards.

All of the programmes and projects in the first version of the Portfolio Schedule and Portfolio Plan should be detailed. Saying, for example, 'It's only a small project, it's not a problem' or 'It's only a small project, we'll do its organization later' is not good enough – this is how problems such as lack of organizational commitment/ownership and un-owned projects happen.

At this stage of portfolio generation it is likely that the BUs and functional areas will raise issues in relation to resource commitment, conflict with existing change initiatives or conflict with operational commitments. This needs to be iterated until the scope, ownership and resourcing of the BU/functional area's portfolio has been agreed. Whilst the commitment to individual programmes and projects may be made by the respective Senior Responsible Owner and Project Executive, the overall BU/functional area's commitment will need to be made by the (Business) Change Manager for the affected/owning area.

Closing the segmentation stage requires the BUs/functional areas signing up to owning and resourcing the programmes and projects and/or raising issue with what can/can't be delivered. This acceptance of ownership should extend to the BUs/functional areas signing up to the (draft/outline) costs and benefits for the projects.

3.7 PROCESS STEP 6 – CONFIRM THE PORTFOLIO STRATEGY, PORTFOLIO SCHEDULE AND PORTFOLIO PLAN

The steps of triangulating the Portfolio Strategy, Portfolio Schedule and Portfolio Plan may well go in several cycles of iteration, review and refinement across many different versions of all three before there is agreement on a unitary triumvirate of Portfolio Strategy, Portfolio Schedule and

Portfolio Plan that will adequately meet the organization's strategic targets and goals, within acceptable levels of spend, risk, organizational commitment and change.

The summaries of the Portfolio Strategy, Portfolio Schedule and Portfolio Plan given below indicate the depth and rigour needed in each to build a valid triangulation, giving an acceptable portfolio.

3.7.1 Content of the Portfolio Strategy

A translation of the organization's strategy, goals and targets into the rules and goals of change initiatives, to include:

- The rules of the process by which the portfolio is built (including the rules of programme and project selection, prioritization, categorization, segmentation etc.)
- A timeline of the expected outcomes of change initiatives at the corporate level, aligned to the strategic goals and targets of the organization
- A first version of the parameters within which the corporate portfolio will be managed (e.g. risk, financial, resource)
- Timelines of the expected outcomes of change initiatives at the BU level and also for the functions, aligned to the strategic goals and targets of the BUs and functions
- A first version of the parameters (e.g. the risk, financial, resource limits) within/for which the changes for that part of the organization (i.e. BUs and functions) will be managed and delivered.

3.7.2 Content of the Portfolio Schedule

Core attributes for each programme or project, to include:

- High-level statement of what the programme/project will deliver
- Programme/project name

- Which parts of the organization the programme/project will impact
- Expected costs
- Delivery timelines (i.e. what, when)
- Segmentation of the programme/project (i.e. in which portfolio/sub-portfolio/programme; confirming the part of the organization where the programme/project will be owned)
- Expected owner of the programme/project
- Categorization of the programme/project
- Priority of the programme/project.

3.7.3 Content of the Portfolio Plan

The delivery schedule of the portfolio (across the programmes and projects of the portfolio):

- Resource profiling
- Cost profiling
- Benefits profiling
- The danger of change overload (too much planning or delivery of change) affecting the organization at any one time
- The scale of (accepted) risk associated with delivering the changes
- Relative prioritization
- Removing possible duplication
- Expected resource scarcity and conflict
- Bottlenecks
- Dependencies
- Business ownership of the programmes and projects
- Any arising risks and issues
- For each programme and project:
  - What organizational/business changes will be delivered, and into which part of the organization
  - When the organizational/business changes will be delivered
  - Which programme or project will deliver which organizational/business changes

- What resources will be used to deliver the changes
- Who will own, deliver and accept the changes.

3.7.4 Sign-off for the Portfolio Strategy, Portfolio Schedule and Portfolio Plan

The process of iteration and refinement across successive drafts of the Portfolio Strategy, Portfolio Schedule and Portfolio Plan will result in the necessary agreed triangulation of the three, with the right balance of strategic alignment, deliverability and risk, and resource consumption. The three should then be signed off/accepted by the Portfolio Board, under advice from the Portfolio Director. The signed-off Portfolio Strategy, Portfolio Schedule and Portfolio Plan act as a baseline for the performance of the portfolio over the forthcoming year (or other planning cycle).

3.8 PROCESS STEP 7 – TRACKING AND ACTION

This is how the delivery of the programmes and projects in the portfolio is monitored to ensure they are on track relative to their business cases, delivery plans and resource utilization plans. This activity does not look at the performance of the portfolio as a whole, but very much at the performance of the individual programmes and projects in the portfolio.

Once the Portfolio Strategy, Portfolio Schedule and Portfolio Plan have been signed off, the portfolio can move into formal delivery (this will have been ongoing for existing projects). As suggested in Section 4.7 'Portfolio planning and control', there will need to be a very clear reporting hierarchy, with the performance of projects, programmes and the portfolio milestones feeding up to, at-least monthly, review by the Portfolio Board or Portfolio Office.

3.8.1 Reporting and board meetings

The Portfolio Board (or at least the Portfolio Director) must make sure that it is up to date with the performance of the programmes and projects in the portfolio. This means monthly upward collation and review from project to portfolio level. Within programmes, and more particularly projects, review points may sometimes be built around deliverables. This means that performance reviews may not take place in a regular and recurrent manner.

Such an approach will not work in a portfolio environment. The Portfolio Board should meet on a formal and regular basis. The greater the degree of transformational change predicated by the portfolio or the greater the aggregate level of risk, the greater will be the need to have formal, visible control over the aggregate change.

Board reporting frequency

Effective portfolio control is built on standardization and regularity of reporting. Below is a tried and well-proven reporting timeline:

1 The projects should report to the programme on a monthly basis with a detailed dashboard or performance update:
   - This monthly report should have been approved by the Project Executive (or by the Project Board, should it sit) before it is passed up to the Programme Board.
   - Although against the PRINCE2 notion of management by exception, many larger organizations with evolved portfolio practices have monthly Project Boards that must take place. In such an environment the Project Boards in a programme would need to sit each month before the Programme Board.
   - It is suggested that Project Boards, should they meet, do so in the first week of each month.

2 The programmes should report performance to the portfolio on a monthly basis with a detailed dashboard or performance update:

- The dashboard should include the performance measures or KPIs that are appropriate for the project, its programme and the portfolio.
- This monthly report should have been approved by the Senior Responsible Owner (or Programme Board should it meet) before it is passed up to portfolio level.
- Although against the MSP notion of management by exception, many larger organizations with evolved portfolio practices have monthly Programme Boards that must take place. In such an environment the Programme Boards in the portfolio would need to sit each month before the Portfolio Board.
- It is suggested that Programme Boards, should they meet, do so in the second week of each month.

3 Those responsible for the portfolio should formally review programme and project performance on a monthly basis:

- The organization may decide to have monthly Portfolio Boards. If so this would be the time and place to for the monthly portfolio level review of programme and project performance.
- If the organization decides to have monthly Portfolio Boards, it is suggested that the Portfolio Board meets in the third week of each month.
- If the organization decides to have less frequent Portfolio Boards, e.g. quarterly, the monthly portfolio-level review of programme and project performance would still need to take place, and may be undertaken by the Portfolio Office and reported to the Portfolio Director.

Reporting frequency and content

The suggested content of the performance reporting listed above is shown in Table 3.5.

3.8.2 Taking corrective action

Should programmes or projects move outside their boundaries or tolerances, action must be taken. The action is taken to ensure that the portfolio as a whole will, via the Portfolio Plan, deliver against the Portfolio Strategy. At this point, and at the programme and project level, the action should be to bring the programmes and projects back to delivering against their business cases, and not to reform the Portfolio Strategy to accommodate any changes in the business cases of the programmes or projects.

The primary actions to be considered are the standard programme and project level actions in assessing adverse impact on a change initiative:

- Can the programme or project be brought back into line without destroying its business case?
- Are the revised cost/scope/time/expected benefits still acceptable?
- Is the revised business case worth pursuing in cost/benefit terms?
- If the revised business case is worth pursuing in cost/benefit terms, is it acceptable in terms of its revised risk profile and organizational impact?

If the answers to the above questions are all 'Yes' then the impacts of the revised business case, delivery plan and Benefits Realization Plan will need to be fed into revising the Portfolio Strategy, Portfolio Schedule and Portfolio Plan. Any such impacts on the Portfolio Strategy and Portfolio Plan would need to be formally accepted by the Portfolio Board.

Table 3.5 Reporting frequency and content

Reporting element	Content
Project reporting – monthly, possibly via the Project Board	Progress against project milestones, deliverables and/or products
	Issues that need addressing
	Updated Project Risk Register and Issues Log (and escalation to Programme Risks Register and Issues Log for risks and issues that cannot be resolved at project level)
	Update on project dependencies (both ways)
	Position in project lifecycle
	RAG (Red Amber Green) status, possibly against a number of criteria (e.g. delivery schedule, resource usage, budget, risk, issues) as well as overall status
	Financial performance in year and over project lifecycle
	Deliverability of benefits
	Actual and expected resource usage
	Outcomes of any audits, reviews or health-checks.
Programme reporting – monthly, possibly via the Programme Board	Progress against programme milestones
	Issues raised from projects that need addressing at programme level
	Updated Programme Risks Register and Issues Log (and escalation to Portfolio Risks Register and Issues Log for risks and issues that cannot be resolved at programme level)
	Update on any programme dependencies (both ways)
	RAG status, possibly against a number of criteria (e.g. delivery schedule, resource usage, budget, risk, issues) as well as overall status
	Financial performance in year and over project lifecycle
	Actual and expected deliverability of benefits, with respect to Programme Business Case
	Actual and expected programme resource usage
	Outcomes of any audits, reviews or health-checks.

Table 3.5 Reporting frequency and content – *continued*

Reporting element	Content
Portfolio review of programmes and projects – quarterly	Actual and expected programme and project performance against business cases
	Progress against milestones in Portfolio Strategy
	Portfolio-level issues that need addressing
	Updated Portfolio Risks Register and Issues Log (and possible escalation to corporate Risks Register and Issues Log for risks and issues that cannot be resolved at portfolio level – Portfolio Risks Register and Issues Log may be part of corporate Risks Register and Issues Log, or they may be one and the same)
	Resolution of issues raised from programmes and projects that need addressing at portfolio level
	Updated Portfolio (corporate?) Risks Register and Issues Log
	Confirm upcoming schedule of any audits, reviews or health-checks.

In taking corrective action, it is important to note that the estimates for projects and especially programmes are often based on a great deal of uncertainty, and often the problems are outside the authority of the project or programme manager, such as a risk agreed at portfolio level which actually happens. There is a risk that taking a heavy-handed approach to resolution results in a blame culture and creates more problems than it solves.

3.9 PROCESS STEP 8 – PORTFOLIO REVIEW AND REPRIORITIZATION

This activity addresses how:

- The portfolio as a whole will be reviewed to ensure it is delivering against the Portfolio Strategy, and
- The Portfolio Strategy is to be reviewed and possibly changed to ensure that it remains aligned to the (changing) strategy of the organization.

3.9.1 Portfolio review

The Portfolio Board should formally review portfolio performance relative to the Portfolio Strategy on an at least quarterly basis (quarterly is suggested as this activity is greater than the, possibly monthly, review of programme and project performance, and will require both the collating of portfolio performance information and the willingness to consider reprioritizing or stopping projects and or programmes). This is the time for ensuring alignment of the portfolio (and reprioritization of the programmes and projects) to the strategy of the organization.

This activity should both collate actual and expected programme and project performance information to give a portfolio view, and dig into the actual and expected performance of individual programmes and projects.

The main themes to be addressed are:

- Confirm the validity of past progress and forecast for programmes and projects
- Confirm the ongoing strategic alignment of the individual programmes and projects
- Confirm that the Portfolio Plan will deliver against the Portfolio Strategy (required financial rates of return and other strategic measures will be met)
- Ensure any new or emerging risk and issues are addressed.

Coming out of this there may be a need to adjust the priority, or even cancel programmes or projects from the portfolio. Any such impacts on the Portfolio Strategy, Portfolio Schedule or Portfolio Plan would need to be formally accepted by the Portfolio Board.

3.9.2 Portfolio reprioritization

At least annually, the Portfolio Board should review the Portfolio Strategy to ensure that it both best reflects the changed needs of the organization's strategy, and is the best way of realizing those changes.

Ensuring that the Portfolio Strategy reflects the changed needs of the organization should be a part of the organization's strategic planning cycle. If the organization has a two-year planning cycle, it may still be appropriate to initiate an annual review of strategic alignment. The reason for suggesting an at-least annual review is that a year is a long time (over which much money and other resource may be expended) before the value and validity of, perhaps scores of, projects is reconfirmed.

The process of reviewing and adjusting the Portfolio Strategy will lead on to reviewing and adjusting the Portfolio Plan and Portfolio Schedule, and also reviewing and possibly adjusting the categorization, prioritization and segmentation of the programmes and projects in the portfolio.

Portfolio governance 4

4   Portfolio governance

4.1   OVERVIEW

This section discusses governance themes for successful portfolio management, noting that governance is the most critical success factor for effective portfolio management. This section outlines the elements that comprise effective portfolio governance.

There may be problems with a particular change initiative because of, for example:

- Too high a level of risk: complexity, uncertainty, scale, timeframe – or any combination of high-risk factors (which requires evidence-based assessment of what is likely to succeed)
- Inappropriate objectives: the initiative is unlikely to deliver the intended outcome (which requires a clear mapping of the intended strategic impact and the likely result)
- Insufficient resources: the organization is over-committed and cannot provide the required resources
- Significant impact on immediate revenue streams associated with BAU; for example the corporation simply cannot afford to implement such radical change initiatives.

4.1.1   Scope of portfolio governance

Decision makers should be provided with the indicators that help them to understand all of the problems outlined above. The governance framework should create involvement and authority at the right levels to ensure:

- Ownership and direction from the top
- The right people in governance roles, with the authority and experience to make effective decisions

- Rigorous screening of programmes and projects for strategic fit and achievability (typically through a corporate investment board)
- Investment appraisal authority and responsibilities are known and understood, i.e. the role of the Portfolio, Programme and Project Boards in agreeing investment at significant review and decision points
- A standard lifecycle management, as it is crucial to have a model of project lifecycle that will apply to all the projects
- Decisive action to stop programmes and projects that are no longer aligned to current priorities – or those that are obviously failing
- Decisions are consistent with and proportionate to the priorities of the organization.

Governance needs to be applied consistently at portfolio, programme and project levels. In understanding what governance structures need to be in place, it is important to note:

- The Portfolio Board is ultimately accountable for ensuring that programmes and projects achieve the required outcomes.
- Membership of the board includes those with a track record of successful delivery
- Levels of accountability are clearly defined and ownership agreed throughout the delivery chain
- Programmes are initiated on a sound basis, aligned with strategic objectives, have clearly defined outcomes, delivery strategy and governance arrangements
- Governance structures take account of cultural fit and practices across organizational boundaries

- Common standards for reporting are consistently applied, across different partners, different programmes and different projects
- The right things are measured across the work streams and managed by exception.

4.1.2 Overview of the elements of portfolio governance

The governance of the portfolio includes areas of MSP (i.e. the Governance Themes) and PRINCE2 (i.e. the Components) that are relevant to ensuring the appropriate governance of the portfolio. Where there may be either overlapping or different MSP/PRINCE2 approaches to particular themes, the need for appropriate portfolio governance takes priority. The governance themes are summarized in Figure 4.1.

The elements of portfolio governance are:

- The portfolio management approach
- Organization
- Integrated programme and project management
- Stakeholder Engagement and Leadership
- Benefits realization
- Planning and control
- Risk management.

Portfolio management approach

- Creation of the aligned Portfolio Control Framework and Change Delivery Framework
- Importance of the Portfolio Strategy to underpin the Portfolio Control Framework and Change Delivery Framework.

Organization

- Portfolio-level roles and responsibilities

Figure 4.1 Elements of portfolio governance

Portfolio Management Approach		
Organization	Integrated programme and project management	Stakeholder Engagement and Leadership
Benefits realization	Planning and control	Risk management

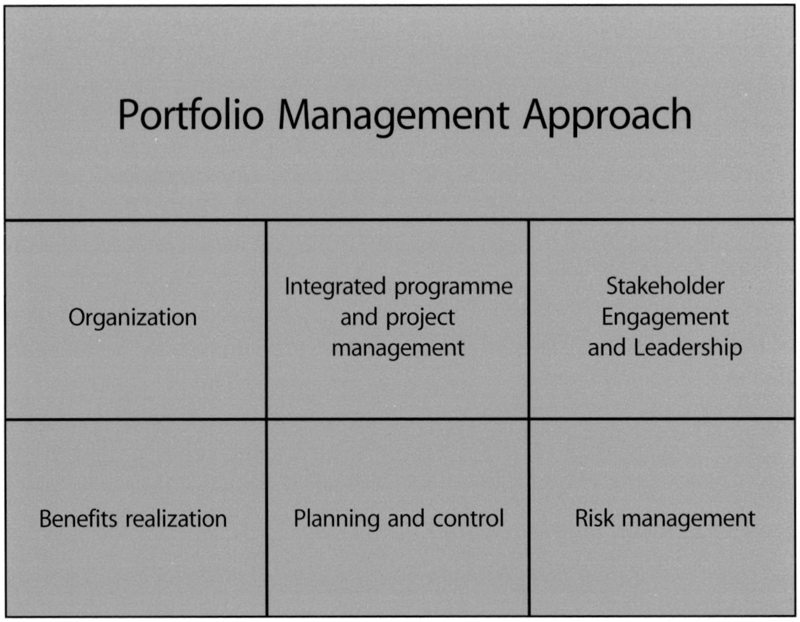

- Coordination across the organization's stakeholder areas, including: directors and senior management, functions (e.g. IT, finance, HR, regulation and policy, risk management), operations and other departments/areas that may be impacted by the portfolio.

Integrated programme and project management

- Content of the change delivery framework:
  - Roles and responsibilities
  - Processes (e.g. approval and escalation processes)
  - Deliverables, covering management, technical and specialist across the portfolio, programmes and projects.

Stakeholder Engagement and Leadership

- How the stakeholders outside the formal Portfolio Organization are to be engaged and involved.

Benefits realization

- How the benefits of the portfolio are to be assured and delivered, down to the level of:
  - Programme and project business case approval (including objectives, scope, sponsorship, ROI, alignment to strategic objectives, dependencies
  - Ensuring project business cases are valid
  - Making sure that realization of benefits is owned by the relevant business area(s) of the organization.

Planning and control

- The standards that will be applied in:
  - Ensuring clear visibility and control of budgets, milestones, dependencies
  - Resource planning, review and allocation
  - Reporting and decision making (to include resolving redundancies and overlaps across projects)
  - Forecasting and acting on these.

Risk management

- Anticipating generic challenges and common issues.

4.2 PORTFOLIO MANAGEMENT APPROACH

For any approach, model, process or activity to add the most value, how it is to add value should be clearly defined. This clarity of definition helps the organization to:

- Make sure that the scope and nature of the model will address its needs, and
- Tailor the model, as needed, to meet its needs on an ongoing basis.

Therefore the organization should list what it wants from its portfolio management approach, and how it will meet this requirement. This approach, once ratified, can be expanded with greater detail of the specific listed individual requirements. Any organizational approach to portfolio management is, at heart, made up of four integrated activities:

- Collecting information: about the current programmes and projects, about organizational capability (level of programme and project management skills) and about current capacity (availability of resources)
- Categorization and analysis: categorizing each programme and project using an agreed set of criteria; analysing the overall complexity and challenge of the portfolio
- Prioritization and decisions: establishing the relative importance of proposed or current programmes and projects and then revisiting those decisions as changes occur in the delivery environment
- Tracking progress and taking action: monitoring the critical aspects of delivery and taking prompt corrective action when required.

To work effectively, the approach must be dynamic – that is, decisions are reviewed and revisited as circumstances change. The portfolio is continually realigned to reflect current priorities. The approach should also cover the 'why', 'what' and 'how' of defining and managing the portfolio in that organization.

There is a clear distinction between managing the portfolio on the one hand and delivering the programmes and projects on the other. Managing the portfolio is an ongoing business-as-usual function, comparable to financial management or control of risk within the organization; it is a permanent activity of the organization. Programmes and projects are temporary activities where the control and delivery standards used on the programmes and projects are those that are provided by the portfolio function. This distinction is reflected in the two frameworks that comprise the portfolio management approach (see Figure 4.2).

- Portfolio Control Framework – scope of the portfolio in terms of expected performance, the programmes and projects that will deliver this, and how this will be delivered
- Change Delivery Framework – how the programmes and projects will be defined, evolved, owned and controlled.

Whilst the Change Delivery Framework is subservient to the Portfolio Control Framework, they must work together to give the required balance of strategic visibility and control (the focus of the Portfolio Control Framework) and visibility and control of the project and programmes of the portfolio (the focus of the Change Delivery Framework).

4.2.1 Portfolio Control Framework

This comprises the Portfolio Strategy, Portfolio Plan and Portfolio Schedule (see Figure 4.3 for greater detail).

Figure 4.2 Portfolio management approach

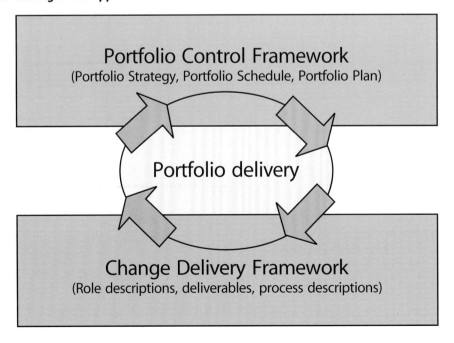

Figure 4.3 Elements of the Portfolio Control Framework

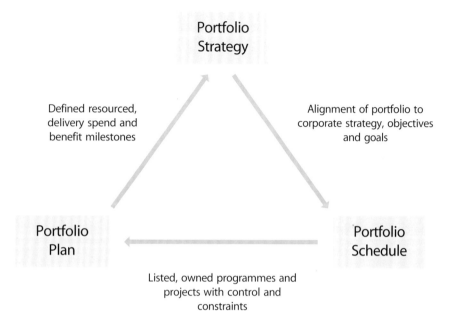

The Portfolio Strategy, Portfolio Plan and Portfolio Schedule form a triangulation confirming:

- Ongoing alignment of the portfolio with corporate objectives and goals (Portfolio Strategy)
- Detailed, owned programmes and projects operating within defined control and constraints (Portfolio Schedule)
- Clear strategic delivery, spend and benefit realization milestones (Portfolio Plan).

4.2.2 Change Delivery Framework

If the programmes and projects are to offer the consistent visibility and control that the portfolio and the Portfolio Control Framework require, the standardization of change activity across the programmes and projects must include:

- Process descriptions
  - Describe the processes that will be used to govern change across the organization

- Should focus on the sanctioning and control processes needed to ensure change is controlled across the organization (e.g. approval and escalation processes).
- Deliverables
  - Describe the deliverables that will be used in the governance of change across the organization
  - Should focus on the management and other deliverables that will be used to ensure change is controlled across the organization (covering management, technical and specialist deliverables across the portfolio, programmes and projects).
- Role descriptions
  - Describe the roles that will be involved in the governance of change across the organization

- Should focus on the roles involved in change needed to ensure change is controlled across the organization through clear accountabilities and responsibilities.

The portfolio should define the controls and standards around the above three, ideally in three separate standards documents, where the process descriptions document makes reference to the roles and deliverables defined in the other two documents. This is shown in Figure 4.4.

4.2.3 Portfolio Strategy

The organizational vision should be a picture of a better future. In portfolio management it is the basis for the outcomes and delivered benefits of the portfolio. It is vital for focus, motivation and activity alignment of the programmes and projects and the large community of people involved across the portfolio.

The Portfolio Strategy is the touchstone against which the other elements of the portfolio management approach should be judged:

- Does the Portfolio Schedule (Portfolio Control Framework) contain the projects and programmes for delivery against the Portfolio Strategy?
- Will the Portfolio Plan (Portfolio Control Framework) deliver against the Portfolio Strategy?
- Do the roles and responsibilities in the roles descriptions (Change Delivery Framework) give adequate and clear ownership of the projects and programmes in the Portfolio Schedule?
- Do the deliverables (Change Delivery Framework) give clarity about what is required to be delivered and/or accepted/rejected?
- Do the process descriptions (Change Delivery Framework) show the sanctioning and control processes with defined, owned deliverables across the portfolio, its programmes and projects?

Figure 4.4 Elements of the Change Delivery Framework

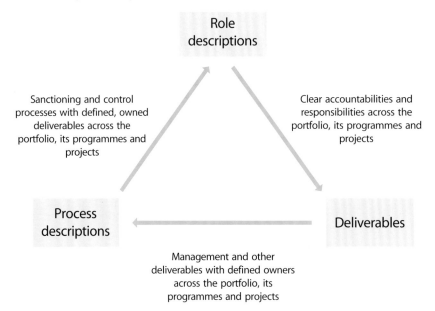

The answer to all the above questions should be 'Yes' for the portfolio management approach to be accepted with its constituent parts adequately interlocking and cross-supporting.

The Portfolio Strategy is used to communicate the goals of the portfolio (and also thereby confirm the alignment of the portfolio to the organization's strategy). The Portfolio Strategy is also therefore a summary impression of the desired future state for the organization. The Portfolio Strategy will describe the performance parameters of the organization in an iterative and evolutionary fashion. Whilst the programmes' Vision Statements describe the new services, improved service levels, etc. to be introduced by the programmes, the Portfolio Strategy sits at a higher level, acting as a time-based aggregation of the organizational performance metrics explicit in the programmes' Vision Statements and Blueprints. This should also include the time-based organizational performance measures explicit in the business case and Benefits Realization Plans of stand-alone projects within the portfolio.

When any organization goes through transformational change, different stakeholders may well benefit from the combination of the description of an organizational vision, or programmes' Vision Statements, and the quantitative roadmap of the Portfolio Strategy.

Characteristics of a good Portfolio Strategy
A good Portfolio Strategy:

- Summarizes the delivery of the transformation agenda of the organization
- Describes the steps to a specified future state (it is time-based, and may be iterative)
- Has a strong quantitative element (it should summarize the corporate-level end and interim states in performance terms (financial, scope and nature of services, customers etc.)

- Is not to be confused with an objective, intention or mission; it is a (possibly iterative) snapshot of the organization in the future
- Can be understood by a wide variety of stakeholders; and it is easy to communicate
- Should avoid jargon understood by only one group, but should contain specific and measurable statements of future organizational performance
- Need not state that the future is better than the present. The Portfolio Strategy is not a marketing or selling tool like an organizational vision or the Vision Statement of a programme. Vis-à-vis a programme, the Portfolio Strategy is in nature closer to the Blueprint (including any intermediate Blueprints)
- Is short and memorable with explicit target dates with explicit target performance levels (numeric targets are the essence of a good Portfolio Strategy)
- Should indicate greater detail via cascade to detailed performance targets at the programme, project and organizational levels.

Developing and maintaining the Portfolio Strategy
It takes time and the involvement of a number of people to draft a clear, effective and inclusive Portfolio Strategy. The 'Defining the Portfolio Strategy' work (see Section 3.2) is the first step in defining, delivering and managing the portfolio and should begin as soon as the Portfolio Director has been appointed and has started building the Portfolio Board. The Portfolio Director would assemble the representative group of executive management to ensure the appropriate corporate ownership and begin building outline Portfolio Strategy options based on the information in the:

- Business requirements (e.g. cascade from organizational vision, to mission, strategies and objectives)
- Programme and project information (information on the in-flight projects and programmes)

- Organizational capability and capacity information (helping to define the resource and risk constraints).

Agreeing the Portfolio Strategy may take several iterations, and several outlines. It is often the case that the draft Portfolio Strategy (including as it does the hard reality of current commitments, e.g. in-flight projects and programmes and organizational constraints, financial and human, related to resources) leads to the organization's initial strategies and objectives being amended and even possibly made less ambitious.

Allowing sufficient time for a good Portfolio Strategy to be developed by the Portfolio Board is critical, as the ongoing steps of the portfolio process (see earlier) will flow from this document.

The Portfolio Strategy should be regularly reviewed during the steps of the portfolio process. Given the importance of the Portfolio Strategy, it should be reviewed formally against the organization's strategy, at a frequency that is aligned to the degree of strategic stability, or otherwise, of the organization. If the strategy of the organization is liable to change, then the Portfolio Strategy must be reviewed more frequently to ensure it is derived from and aligned to the strategy of the organization. For many organizations this corresponds to an annual detailed review and top-down/bottom-up portfolio rebuild (as part of the planning and budgeting cycle). Alongside this, there should be an at-least quarterly review of the portfolio to ensure ongoing strategic alignment.

The Portfolio Strategy should be regarded as a constant and stable foundation for the portfolio. If the Portfolio Strategy does require major changes, it:

- Risks confusing stakeholders, possibly even undermining the credibility of the portfolio
- Could indicate that the portfolio is no longer strategically aligned, and that a detailed review and top-down/bottom-up portfolio rebuild may be required

- May mean review and change to the other elements of the Portfolio Control Framework and possibly the Change Delivery Framework.

4.2.4 Roles and responsibilities

Role	Responsibilities
Portfolio Board	Contribute to the development of the Portfolio Control Framework
	Approve the content of the Portfolio Control Framework
	Commit to supporting the delivery of the performance targets described and the implicit transformation of the Portfolio Control Framework
	Authorize any changes to the Portfolio Control Framework.
Portfolio Director	Develop the Portfolio Control Framework and the Change Delivery Framework
	Gain Portfolio Board and other senior support to the Portfolio Control Framework
	Ensure that the organization is capable of delivering the performance targets described and achieving the implicit transformation of the Portfolio Control Framework
	Ensure that the Change Delivery Framework supports the Portfolio Control Framework
	Implement the Change Delivery Framework against/via programmes and projects
	Lead the delivery of, and maintain focus on, the Portfolio Strategy by the programmes and projects of the portfolio
	Plan and deliver any required changes to the Change Delivery Framework.

4.3 ORGANIZATION

Establishing a clear and effective organization is critical to portfolio success. Ensuring that the Portfolio Organization meets the needs of the portfolio in its context is an initial and ongoing task; whilst programmes and projects are temporary affairs (although it often may not seem like this!), managing the portfolio is an operational/business-as-usual activity. The projects and programmes will come and go, but the portfolio is the ongoing vehicle for ensuring their prioritization, coordination and delivery.

Effective Portfolio Organization means the combination of:

- Defined roles
- Clear responsibilities of each of these roles
- Management structures and reporting arrangements;

that is needed for the portfolio to deliver against its performance targets (as defined in its Portfolio Strategy). The roles, responsibilities and structures discussed below provide the basis for effective portfolio management. They will need to be tailored to suit individual portfolios.

4.3.1 Portfolio leadership

Portfolios take and combine strategic objectives by translating them into a set of prioritized, concrete targets that are delivered against by the individual programmes and projects. The portfolio provides the bridge between strategic objectives and programmes and projects.

The principles for effective leadership of a portfolio that fall to the members of the Portfolio Board (including the Portfolio Director and the Senior Responsible Owners of the programmes) are:

- Vision delivering, showing an ability to deliver the beneficial future that is contained in the organization's vision and the programmes' Vision Statements

- Flexibility to manage, adjust and change to best deliver the performance targets in the Portfolio Strategy
- Empowered decision making, giving individuals (e.g. the programmes' Senior Responsible Owners) the autonomy to fulfil their roles effectively. Motivation, reward and appraisal systems are vital for fostering the attitudes and energy to drive the portfolio
- Visible commitment and authority to:
  - Ensure the correct resources are available to the portfolio (taking into account the relative priority of the programmes and projects in the portfolio)
  - Balance the portfolio's priorities with those of the ongoing business operations
  - Focus on realization of the business benefits and delivery of the underlying transformational changes of the Portfolio Strategy
- Relevant skills and experience to provide direction in the active management of:
  - The prioritization and strategic alignment of the programmes and projects of the portfolio
  - The portfolio's resources (e.g. financial, HR, assets and infrastructure) and the inevitable conflicting demands on resources across the portfolio
  - The coordination of the programmes and projects within the portfolio to see through the transitions to new operational services, while ensuring business operations are maintained
  - Risks, assumptions, issues and dependencies (RAID) across the programmes and projects of the portfolio.

Championing the implementation of the new capabilities delivered by a particular programme must be balanced to ensure that expected benefits are realized and the desired outcomes achieved across the programmes of the portfolio, without undue or unbalanced focus on the delivery of the outcomes of one programme at the expense of another, i.e. ensuring the alignment of the portfolio to the organization's strategic agenda.

4.3.2 Portfolio Organization

Effective leadership of the portfolio can only be achieved through informed decision making and a structured yet flexible management culture. As the portfolio is concerned with deciding on and managing the aggregate sum of change across the organization, the team to run and be accountable for this is self-selecting – it is the senior management of the organization. Alongside this, it is important to ensure the right balance of knowledge and skills in a structure that lets them carry out their roles and contribute their knowledge effectively.

Figure 4.5 shows the core executive groups and how they relate to each other in managing the portfolio. For example, the Project Executive chairs the Project Board

and represents the project at the Programme Board. Likewise the Programme Senior Responsible Owner chairs the Programme Board and represents the programme at the Portfolio Board. The following sections describe the generic responsibilities at the portfolio level, together with the specific roles and the skills that the individuals fulfilling them will need (there will need to be corresponding detail and clarity for the programme and project roles in the portfolio).

4.3.3 Portfolio Board

The Portfolio Board represents the most senior management of the organization, who are responsible for:

- The stewardship of the organization
- Definition and delivery of the strategy of the organization
- Ensuring the ongoing operations of the organization

Figure 4.5 Layering of Portfolio Organization, control and reporting

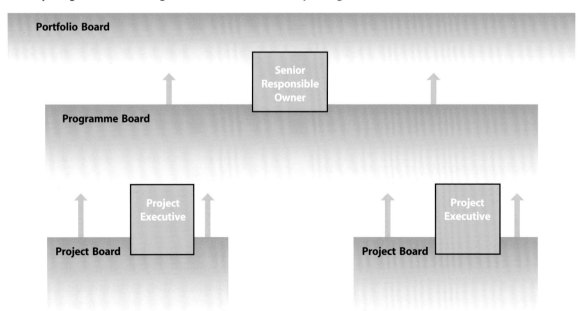

- Best and appropriate usage of the organization's resources and assets
- Ensuring the ongoing overall alignment of the portfolio to the strategic direction of the organization.

The Portfolio Board will appoint the Portfolio Director who, as part of the Portfolio Board, is likely to be a peer of the other members of the Portfolio Board. The role of the Portfolio Board may well be performed by an existing executive committee or board of the organization. The Portfolio Board is the head committee/board of the organization's portfolio management, and is also responsible for the portfolio coming into existence. The Portfolio Strategy, as owned and taken forward by the Portfolio Director, will be agreed by the Portfolio Board. The members of the Portfolio Board will provide resource and specific commitment to support the Portfolio Director, who is accountable for the successful delivery of the projects and programmes in the Portfolio Schedule according to the Portfolio Plan, meeting the performance targets of the Portfolio Strategy.

Responsibilities of the Portfolio Board

- Establishing the organizational and strategic context for the portfolio
- Confirming the organization's strategic direction, against which the portfolio is to deliver
- Authorizing the Portfolio Strategy
- Agreeing the composition, risk profile, and delivery schedule defined both explicitly and implicitly by the Portfolio Control Framework
- Approving funding for the portfolio
- Resolving strategic and directional conflicts between programmes that need the input and agreement of senior stakeholders to ensure the progress of the portfolio
- Approving the delivery of the portfolio against the performance targets of the Portfolio Strategy

- Leading by example the end-state values implied by the organization's vision, and the transformational changes of the programmes within the portfolio
- Providing continued commitment and endorsement in support of the portfolio objectives at executive and communications events
- Advising and supporting the Portfolio Director.

Individually, each member of the Portfolio Board will provide and commit to the Portfolio Director for some or all of the following as appropriate for the area they represent:

- Understanding and managing the impact of change in their functional and/or operational area
- Owning the resolution of risks and issues that the portfolio faces, where resolution may lie in their functional and/or operational area
- Committing functional and/or operational areas to supporting strategy as expressed in, for example, medium-term plans, operational blueprints and the Portfolio Strategy etc.
- Supporting the congruence of operating and portfolio standards.

Membership of the Portfolio Board

The following should be considered as standing members of the Portfolio Board:

- Portfolio Director (see below)
- CEO
- Operations Director
- Senior Responsible Owners of the programmes in the Portfolio Schedule
- Senior representatives of corporate functions (ideally the directors of IT, strategy, finance, risk, HR etc.)

- Partners/Suppliers:
  - If there are different senior suppliers across the programmes and projects of the portfolio, it may be desirable to appoint a lead supplier to work with and through at the portfolio level – whether this will be acceptable to the non-lead supplier is a moot point
  - The organization may alternatively want the Portfolio Board as internal to the organization (with no external members) as it is concerned with the organization's strategic objectives and the benefits, costs, and prioritizing of programmes and projects.

Additional portfolio roles

The following additional portfolio roles should be considered, though they may be part time over the portfolio's life:

- **Risk manager** to provide expertise and management support for risk and issue management
- **Portfolio accountant** to support and ensure compliance to corporate accounting procedures, also provides useful support in business case development
- **Benefits Realization Manager** to provide assurance and overview of the programmes' Benefits Realization Plans and the overall expected benefits delivery of the portfolio. An element of this role is to ensure that there is no overlap between individually owned profiles across the programmes. This should sit at the corporate level to give visibility across the whole portfolio of change, and ensure both achievability and non-duplication across the portfolio. This role would provide assurance against the programme role of the Business Change Manager.

- **Procurement expertise** should be involved early to ensure compliance to corporate strategies and alliances and provide advice. Most portfolios will involve some aspect of procurement.

Portfolio Board formality

The Portfolio Board should meet on a formal and regular basis. The greater the degree of transformational change predicated by the portfolio or the greater the aggregate level of risk, the greater will be the need to have formal, visible control over the changes.

Members of the Portfolio Board must take the lead in establishing a style of leadership appropriate to the organization and the nature of the changes implied by the Portfolio Strategy.

If the organization decides to have Portfolio Boards on an other-than-monthly basis (e.g. quarterly), the monthly portfolio-level review of programme and project performance would still need to take place, and may be undertaken by the Portfolio Office and reported to the Portfolio Director.

The Portfolio Board should meet at least quarterly to confirm the direction and delivery of the portfolio. The portfolio together with the Portfolio Strategy should be rigorously reviewed, with reconfirmation of the organization's strategy and goals, reassessment of programme and project priority, and reformulation of the Portfolio Strategy, Portfolio Schedule and Portfolio Plan on an at-least-yearly basis.

4.3.4 Portfolio Director

The Portfolio Director is accountable to the Portfolio Board for the day-to day performance of the portfolio and its delivery against the Portfolio Strategy, ensuring that it meets its objectives and realizes the expected benefits. The individual who fulfils this role should also be able to advise the Portfolio Board with energy and drive, and must be empowered to direct the portfolio and take decisions. They must have enough seniority, authority and large-scale change expertise to provide leadership and guidance to the Portfolio Board and take on accountability for delivery.

Responsibilities of the Portfolio Director

The Portfolio Director is accountable for the day-to-day success of the portfolio and is responsible for ensuring:

- The portfolio of programmes and projects is achievable, and aligned to corporate objectives and strategic targets
- There are clear relative priorities and interdependencies of the programmes and projects, and the implications of these are understood and accepted
- The resources and skills implications of the portfolio are understood, accepted and acted on
- Assessment of risks and the likelihood of delivery of outcomes/benefits, and that this level of risk is understood and accepted
- Clear understanding of the linkages with external delivery-chain partners
- Clarity across the coordinated demands on resource from operational businesses and identified impact of business change
- Reporting on the performance and RAID of the portfolio to enable the Portfolio Board to make informed decisions
- The portfolio delivers within its agreed parameters (e.g. cost, organizational impact and rate/scale adoption, expected/actual benefits realization)
- Strategic and directional issues that need the input and agreement of senior stakeholders to ensure the progress of the portfolio (e.g. between programmes and projects) are resolved
- The integrity of Benefit Profiles and Realization Plans and ensuring that there is no double counting of benefits.

To deliver against this, the Portfolio Director:

- Owns the vision for the portfolio (the Portfolio Strategy as defined and ratified by the Portfolio Board)
- Leads the portfolio, providing clear leadership and direction throughout its life
- Advises the Portfolio Board on the investment required to set up and run the portfolio, including any transition activities to ensure the desired benefits are realized
- Provides overall direction and leadership for the design, management and delivery of the portfolio
- Is accountable for the portfolio's governance arrangements (to include those for programmes and projects in the Change Delivery Framework)
- Advises the Portfolio Board of the strategic risks facing the portfolio, and possible mitigation of these
- Maintains the alignment of the portfolio to the organization's strategic direction.
- Defines an acceptable risk profile (and risk thresholds for the portfolio and its constituent programmes and projects) and advises the Portfolio Board of portfolio performance against this
- Ensures assurance of operational stability of delivered change, and effectiveness through the ongoing delivery of the portfolio.

Attributes of a Portfolio Director

- Has the seniority for the responsibilities and accountabilities the role involves
- Is proactive and visible as the driving force behind the portfolio
- Strong leadership and decision-making skills
- Experience, character and personality that are right for the portfolio
- Combines realism with openness and the clarity of expression to communicate the portfolio's vision effectively

- Able to give purpose and direction to the portfolio and take strategic decisions
- Focuses on delivery of the benefits and realizing the end goal
- Builds productive relationships across the Portfolio Board
- Has access to and credibility with the most senior management of the organization and other stakeholders.

Given the high level of personal responsibility that the Portfolio Director takes for the portfolio, this person will want to ensure that those on the Portfolio Board are able to contribute and support the portfolio with comparable levels of authority, commitment and ability.

4.3.5 Roles and responsibilities

The following is a summary of the responsibilities for the delivery of an effective Portfolio Organization:

Role	Responsibilities
Portfolio Board	Contribute to the development of the Portfolio Organization
	Approve the content of the Portfolio Organization and the associated documents
	Confirm understanding of their collective and their individual, relative roles and responsibilities.
Portfolio Director	Ensure that the portfolio team has the necessary skills and experience required to deliver the changes across the portfolio
	Ensure that the Portfolio Organization is structured (with the appropriate roles and responsibilities) with the necessary visibility, control and accountability to give confidence in the validity of the business cases, and the deliverability of the programmes and projects in the portfolio
	Ensure that Portfolio Board members have a clear understanding of their roles

Role	Responsibilities
	Design and appointment of the Portfolio Team/Office
	Ensure all roles have clearly defined responsibilities
	Efficient use of resources, and the effective performance of the portfolio.
Portfolio Office	Maintenance of information
	Advice and guidance on roles and responsibilities
	Support in recruitment and appointments.

Greater detail of how the portfolio, programme and project roles work together as an integrated organization linking the accountabilities and responsibilities, within a defined portfolio structure, is explored further in the next section.

4.4 INTEGRATED PROGRAMME AND PROJECT MANAGEMENT

There is a clear distinction between managing the portfolio on the one hand and delivering the programmes and projects on the other. Managing the portfolio is an ongoing business-as-usual function, comparable to financial management or control of risk within the organization; it is a permanent activity of the organization. Programmes and projects are temporary activities where the control and delivery standards used on the programmes and projects are those that are provided by the Portfolio function.

If the programmes and projects are to offer the consistent visibility and control that the portfolio and the Portfolio Control Framework require, the standardization of change activity across the programmes and projects must include:

- Process descriptions
  - Describes the processes that will be used to govern change across the organization.

- Should focus on the high-level sanctioning and control processes needed to ensure change is controlled across the organization (e.g. approval and escalation processes).
- ▪ Deliverables
  - Describes the deliverables that will be used in the governance of change across the organization.
  - Should focus on the management and other deliverables that will be used to ensure change is controlled across the organization (covering management, technical and specialist deliverables across the portfolio, programmes and projects).
- ▪ Role descriptions
  - Describes the roles that will be involved in the governance of change across the organization
  - Should focus on the roles involved in change needed to ensure change is controlled across the organization through clear accountabilities and responsibilities.

The portfolio should define the controls and standards around the above three, ideally in three separate but linked standards documents, where the process standards document (focused on the high-level sanctioning and control processes needed to ensure change is controlled across the portfolio) makes reference to the roles and deliverables defined in the other two documents. The combination of these three control documents is the Change Delivery Framework. This is shown in Figure 4.4.

4.4.1 Portfolio structures

Single-portfolio structure

The basic portfolio hierarchy of the programmes and projects within a portfolio that allows for stand-alone projects to report directly at the portfolio level is shown in Figure 1.1. This is not unexpected for key strategic projects. This hierarchy allows the structured up and down information flows that are necessary if any arising issues are to be debated freely and risks evaluated openly. Making the most of this hierarchy requires a leadership style and culture that encourages the flow of information between projects, programmes and the portfolio. Continuity and stability of the Portfolio Organization structure are also important to ensure that commitment to the portfolio is maintained.

Multiple-portfolio structure

In a multiple-portfolio environment (where the organization or a part of it is running more than one change portfolio at a time), there is a need to coordinate across portfolios to ensure cohesive strategic alignment and prioritization. There must therefore be a clear hierarchy of portfolios, programmes and projects. This is shown in Figure 4.6.

Even in the multi-portfolio hierarchy, there should be allowance for stand-alone projects that report directly at the appropriate portfolio level. As said before, this is not unexpected for key strategic projects.

The existence of a portfolio means the needs for ownership of and responsibility for strategic alignment, prioritization and resource management across a group of programmes and projects. In Figure 4.6 the head portfolio might be the group portfolio in a large organization. Here group-level projects and programmes may be conceived, owned and run. Here also will be the collation, rolling up and reporting of sub-portfolios and their programmes and projects.

The sub-portfolios may be the portfolios of the directorates/business units in the organization/group. These sub-portfolios would be responsible for the strategic alignment, prioritization and resource management across the programmes and projects in that portfolio, as well as delivery against their responsibilities in the group-level programmes and projects.

Figure 4.6 Hierarchy in a multiple-portfolio environment

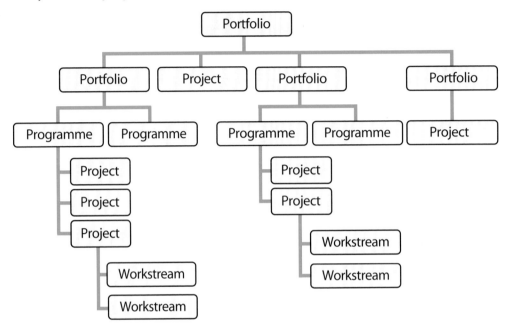

At whatever portfolio level, portfolio ownership means defining the portfolio objectives (the Portfolio Strategy), making the investment decisions and providing the rationale for the balance and focus of the portfolio (in relation to other possible portfolios, profiles and investments), and delivering against the Portfolio Strategy.

Implementing and managing the portfolio structure

There is no single portfolio structure that will fit every type of portfolio. Each portfolio should be directed and managed with the appropriate level of management resources to facilitate clear direction setting and effective management of ongoing progress, but without incurring excessive management overheads.

The portfolio structure will have to meet needs that include:

■ The level of integration and overlap required with programme and project organizations

■ The need to possibly split the responsibilities of the core portfolio roles across more than one individual to cope with large-scale or multiple portfolios

■ The requirement for building cross-organization structures, where the portfolio(s) may span highly autonomous or independent organizations.

It is critical that the Portfolio Organization is empathetic with the organization culture, and careful consideration is given to how it interfaces and merges with other corporate groups and initiatives so that boundaries are clear.

4.4.2 Aligning MSP and PRINCE2 within the portfolio

The sections below explore aspects of integrating MSP and PRINCE2 within a portfolio framework. The models and ideas presented are not rules, and not exhaustive. It is possible that some people may find that the approaches are not sufficiently in accord with what they understand to be the rules of MSP or PRINCE2. They are approaches that have proven to be effective and pragmatic in using MSP for programmes and PRINCE2 for projects in a portfolio environment.

A high-level and simplistic view of how project control fits within programme control, and programme control fits within portfolio control is shown in Figure 4.7.

4.4.3 Using MSP as the main delivery vehicle

The approach in this document assumes that programmes are the primary vehicle for change delivery, and that Managing Successful Programmes will be used as the standard method for programme management. As such the high-level processes from MSP will be core to the management of change. In assuming that programmes

will be the prime delivery mechanism for major initiatives, projects become sub-components of a programme, managed by the PRINCE2 standard method for Project Management; therefore, in cases where the initiative is a single project, the PRINCE2 high-level processes should be substituted in place of the MSP processes as shown in Table 4.1.

The PRINCE2 processes Planning and Managing Product Delivery are not detailed here. In addition, if stand-alone projects are to be allowed at the portfolio level, some of the activities (and possible sub-processes) associated with successful programmes described later would also need to be included as PRINCE2 does not include them. This would include stakeholder management, communication and benefits management during the project.

Figure 4.7 Integration of MSP and PRINCE2 in a portfolio environment

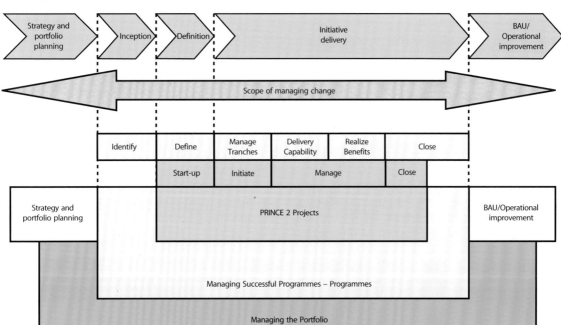

Table 4.1 PRINCE2 processes to be substituted for MSP processes in a stand-alone project

Managing Successful Programmes	PRINCE2 process to be substituted
Identifying a Programme	Starting Up a Project
Defining a Programme	Initiating a Project
Managing the Tranches	Delivering the Capability
Realizing the Benefits	Directing a Project
Controlling a Stage and Managing Product Delivery	Managing Stage Boundaries
Closing a Programme	Closing a Project

4.4.4 Alignment of programme (MSP) and project (PRINCE2) organization

In this section, with a little tweaking, the programme organization from MSP and the project organization from PRINCE2 are used. There are some slight extensions to the organizations for the programmes and projects, to ensure that the reporting and control will work in a portfolio environment. These are:

For Programmes:

- The Programme Manager is part of the Programme Board
- The Senior Responsible Owner owns the Programme Business Case
- The Senior Responsible Owner represents their programme on the Portfolio Board
- Sometimes the Senior Responsible Owner may be represented on the Portfolio Board by the Business Change Manager (delegating to the Programme Manager is more problematic due to the inherent differences in the responsibilities of the Senior Responsible Owner and the Programme Manager).

- The Business Change Manager should sign off the Programme Business Case as achievable (with clearly realizable benefits, a suitably developed Benefits Realization Plan, and appropriate business-as-usual operational ownership) before it goes forward to the Portfolio Board for approval. As new projects are started in the programme, this may mean the programme's business case needing to be reviewed and re-approved on several occasions
- The programme's Business Change Manager reports into the (ideally financial or benefits) assurance function (or Benefits Realization Manager/portfolio accountant should they exist) in the Portfolio team that supports the Portfolio Director
- As an assurance of the validity of the Programme Business Case, and that the benefits will be delivered, the programme's Business Change Manager should never report to either the Programme Manager or the Senior Responsible Owner.

For projects:

- The Project Manager is part of the Project Board
- The Project Executive owns the Programme Business Case

- The Project Executive represents their project on the Programme Board (sometimes the Project Executive may be represented at this by the Change Manager, but ideally not the Project Manager)
- If the importance of a project merits it (due to strategic importance, level of cost, risk, external profile, regulatory compliance, possible reputational damage etc.), the project has its own Change Manager. The role of the project Change Manager is akin to that of the programme Business Change Manager and is responsible for making sure benefits are delivered
- The Change Manager (or senior user if there is no Change Manager on the project) should sign off the Project Business Case as achievable (with clearly realizable benefits, a suitably developed Benefits Realization Plan, and appropriate business-as-usual operational ownership) before it goes forward to be part of Programme Business Case and that is taken forward to the Portfolio Board for approval
- For stand-alone projects in the portfolio, the Change Manager should sign off the Project Business Case as achievable (with clearly realizable benefits, a suitably developed Benefits Realization Plan, and appropriate business-as-usual operational ownership) before it goes forward to the Portfolio Board for approval
- The project's Change Manager reports to the programme's Business Change Manager
- As an assurance of the validity of the Project Business Case, and that the benefits will be delivered, the project's Change Manager should never report to either the Project Manager or the Project Executive.

Projects in programmes in the portfolio

The organization for projects in programmes in the portfolio is given in Figure 4.8.

Stand-alone projects in the portfolio

The organization for stand-alone projects in the portfolio is given in Figure 4.9.

Designing the appropriate levels of engagement between the portfolio, the programmes and the projects is a part of establishing an effective Portfolio Organization. Project-level organization structures need to have clear leadership, direction setting, decision making and management, whether they are operating within a programme or stand-alone. As shown in Figure 4.9, there must be clear responsibilities and reporting that give the visibility, control and accountability for the most senior management of the organization to have confidence in the validity and deliverability of the programmes and projects in the portfolio.

4.4.5 Portfolio focus on programme costs and benefits

Although the controls for programme and project management are defined at the portfolio level, they are enacted at the programme and project level. Thus the attention to delivery of programmes and projects and the day-to-day control of programmes and projects is with the programmes and projects. At the portfolio level the focus will be on the costs and benefits of the programmes and projects, and the timings of these.

Figure 4.10 makes reference to programme and subsidiary project deliverables (e.g. Stage 1 Business Case, Benefits Realization Plan) and activities (e.g. Benefits Measuring & Monitoring, and Quarterly Checkpoint Review) that the portfolio will need to ensure happen and possibly monitor to ensure the initial rigour and ongoing viability of the Programme and Project Business Cases.

Later in this section, there are examples of how the portfolio can keep visibility of programme and project costs and benefits, whilst at the same time allowing flexibility in terms of the nature and scale of governance

Figure 4.8 Organization for projects in programmes in the portfolio

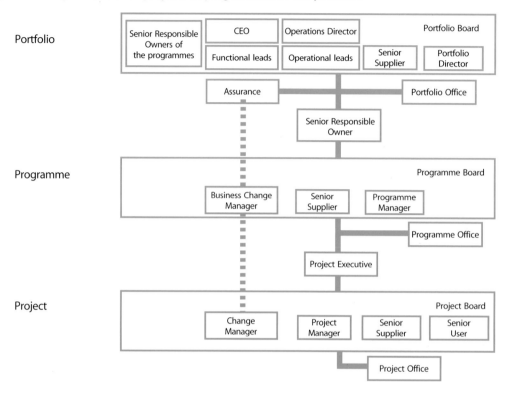

Figure 4.9 Organization for stand-alone projects in the portfolio

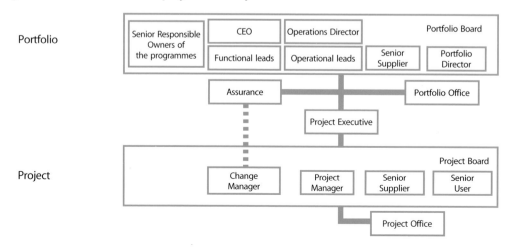

that is applied to projects of different scale (e.g. expected lifetime cost, level of risk, complexity).

4.4.6 Tailoring the approach to change initiatives of different scale

With adopting both MSP and more particularly PRINCE2 there is a risk of bureaucracy and overkill – too much paperwork and process. This is especially true with smaller and quicker projects that do not have a high-risk profile. In tailoring MSP and PRINCE2 to accommodate projects of different scale, it is important that deliverables/products and controls remain, so that the portfolio keeps the visibility that it needs. Although a project may be of low cost or short-term duration, it may still be high risk, possibly amending systems/infrastructure, and offering the scope for major reputational damage.

Figures 4.11 to 4.13 offer one approach for tailoring the level of governance and management deliverables. The indicator used here to set the level of applied governance is the expected lifetime cost of the project. It is possibly to construct a more comprehensive model, where a combination of indicators (e.g. cost, level of risk, technical complexity, degree of stakeholder challenge) are used to assess the level and scale of governance required for the project.

Figure 4.10 Portfolio visibility of programme costs and benefits

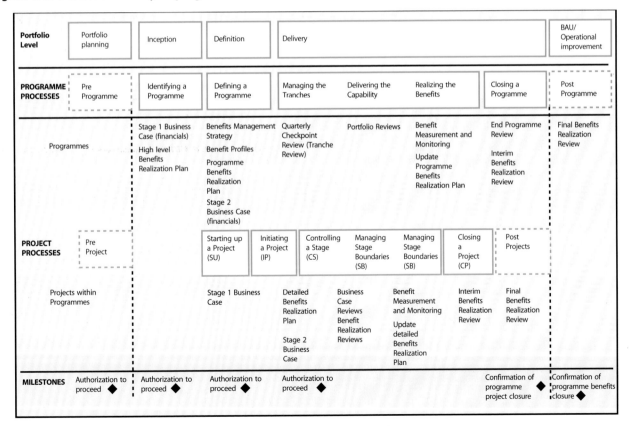

The figures show the suggested management deliverables and milestone controls for projects with an expected lifetime cost of:

- Over £1m – *significant projects*

- £250k to £1m – *standard projects*
- Under £250K – *small projects*.

Of course the value boundaries used for any right-sizing or approach will depend on the balance and spread of

Figure 4.11 Management products and control points in significant projects

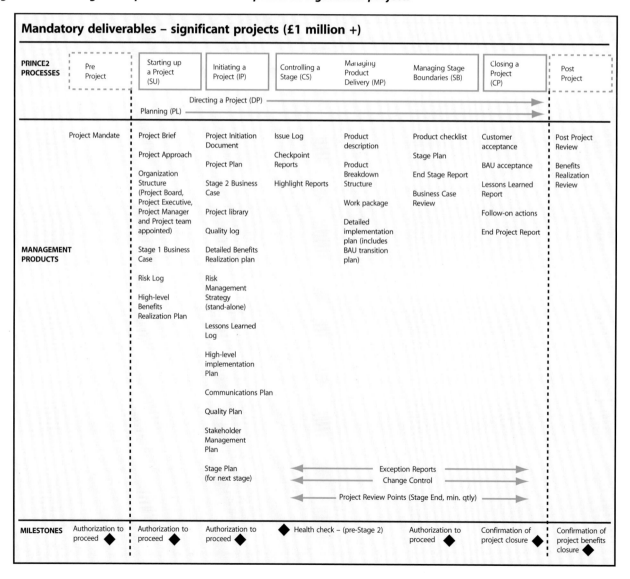

investment values of the programmes and projects in the portfolio.

Figure 4.14 shows portfolio visibility of costs and benefits for *right-sized* projects. It demonstrates the financial- and

benefits-focused management products and controls that the portfolio would want to apply (in the right-sizing approach to governance) to ensure the initial rigour and ongoing viability of the Project Business Cases. This would apply for projects in programmes and stand-alone projects.

Figure 4.12 Management products and control points in standard projects

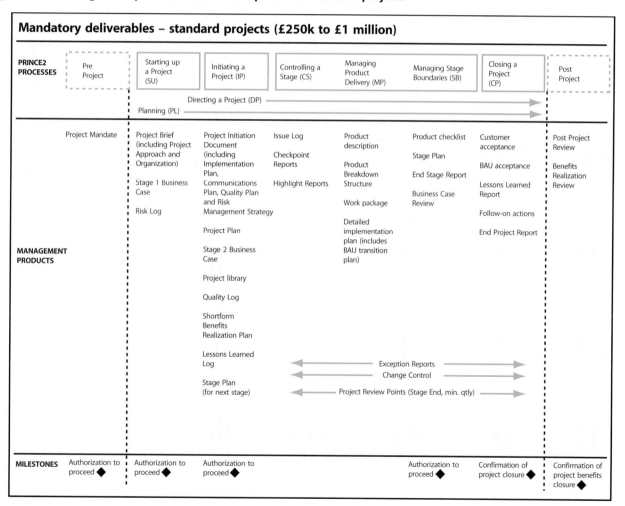

Figure 4.13 Management products and control points in small projects

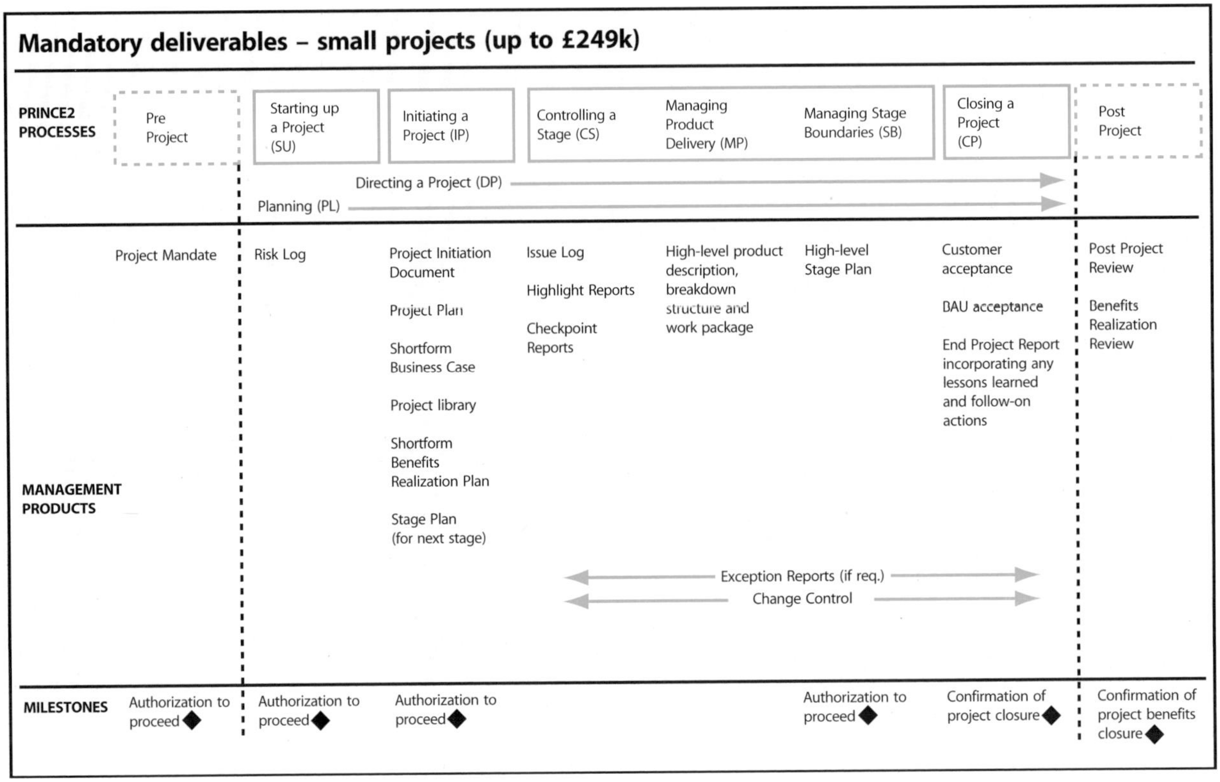

Mandatory deliverables – small projects (up to £249k)							

PRINCE2 PROCESSES

Pre Project	Starting up a Project (SU)	Initiating a Project (IP)	Controlling a Stage (CS)	Managing Product Delivery (MP)	Managing Stage Boundaries (SB)	Closing a Project (CP)	Post Project

Directing a Project (DP) →

Planning (PL)

MANAGEMENT PRODUCTS

Project Mandate	Risk Log	Project Initiation Document	Issue Log	High-level product description, breakdown structure and work package	High-level Stage Plan	Customer acceptance	Post Project Review
		Project Plan	Highlight Reports			BAU acceptance	Benefits Realization Review
		Shortform Business Case	Checkpoint Reports			End Project Report incorporating any lessons learned and follow-on actions	
		Project library					
		Shortform Benefits Realization Plan					
		Stage Plan (for next stage)					

← Exception Reports (if req.) →

← Change Control →

MILESTONES

Authorization to proceed ◆	Authorization to proceed ◆	Authorization to proceed ◆			Authorization to proceed ◆	Confirmation of project closure ◆	Confirmation of project benefits closure ◆

Should the portfolio team wish to adopt a right-sizing approach, it should construct a categorization of applied governance that is right for the portfolio and the organization. The categorization of applied governance that the portfolio team adopts would be one of the groups of category used in the categorizing of the programme and projects in the portfolio.

4.4.7 Incorporating non-management controls

MSP and PRINCE2 address strongly the governance needs of programmes and projects. Management products, processes and stages ensure generic governance is applied. However, the governance needs of a portfolio are

likely to be broader. Specific categories of programmes and projects will need additional deliverables and additional controls.

The portfolio would need to list and define the deliverables and controls that would apply generically (i.e. to all programmes or projects) and also those that would apply to specific categories.

One of the core values of the portfolio is to pull together and assimilate the different controls, deliverables and assessments (e.g. operational impact, risk, change management, IT, business continuity) that need to be applied to programmes and projects. The outcome should be a programme and project delivery model that has the

Figure 4.14 Portfolio visibility of costs and benefits for right-sized projects

Mandatory products and controls for right-sized projects

PROJECT PROCESSES	Pre Project	Starting up a Project (SU)	Initiating a Project (IP)	Controlling a Stage (CS)	Managing Product Delivery (MP)	Managing Stage Boundaries (SB)	Closing a Project (CP)	Post Project
Significant Projects (£1m+)		Stage 1 Business Case Benefits Realization Plan	Benefits Management Strategy Detailed Benefits Realization Plan Stage 2 Business Case	Business Case Reviews Benefits Realization Reviews (part of Highlight Reporting)		Benefits measurement and monitoring Update detailed Benefits Realization Plan	Interim Benefits Realization Review	Final Benefits Realization Review
Standard Projects (£250k to £1m+)		Stage 1 Business Case High-level Benefits Realization Plan	Benefits Realization Plan Stage 2 Business Case	Business Case Reviews Benefits Realization Reviews (part of Highlight Reporting)		Benefits measurement and monitoring Update detailed Benefits Realization Plan	Interim Benefits Realization Review	Final Benefits Realization Review
Small Projects (up to £249k)			Shortform Benefits Realization Plan Shortform Stage 2 Business Case	Business .Case Reviews Benefits Realization Reviews (part of Highlight Reporting)		Benefits measurement and monitoring Update Shortform Benefits Realization Plan		Final Benefits Realization Review
MILESTONES	Authorization to proceed ◆	Authorization to proceed ◆	Authorization to proceed ◆			Authorization to proceed ◆	Confirmation of project closure ◆	Confirmation of project benefits closure ◆

controls, deliverables and assessments embedded into the programme and project lifecycles. The value of this is greater clarity and efficiency in the application of the right control over the programme and project lifecycles.

For many organizations, IT projects may form a high percentage of the projects that they undertake. IT projects need deliverables and controls around data standards, IT strategy, IT architecture, applications integration etc. Therefore the programmes and projects that fall within the IT category would need to adhere to these controls. The application of these controls would need to be aligned to the project management lifecycle. A generic set of IT category deliverables and controls, aligned to the PRINCE2 lifecycle, are shown in Figure 4.15.

Figure 4.15 Example of generic IT controls for a project

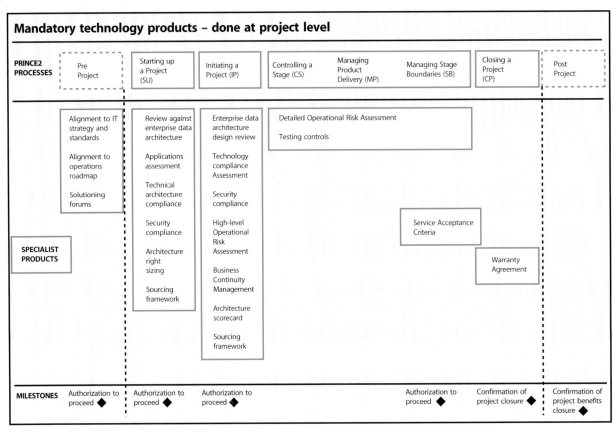

4.4.8 Roles and responsibilities

The following is a summary of the responsibilities for the integration of programme and project management within the portfolio:

Role	Responsibilities
Portfolio Board	Contribute requirements to the content of the roles, process and deliverables documents, and the development of the integration of programme and project management
	Confirm their understanding and acceptance of the visibility and control that the integration of programme and project management gives them
	Approve the roles, process and deliverables documents that constitute the integration of programme and project management
	Report to the organization's management or executive board for ultimate sanction.
Portfolio Director	Ensures that the portfolio has the necessary skills and experience required to deliver against the integration of programme and project management
	Ensures that the Portfolio Organization is structured (with the appropriate roles and responsibilities) to deliver and support the integration of programme and project management
	Ensures that Portfolio Board members have a clear understanding of their roles and responsibilities
	Ensures that the Portfolio Office is structured and skilled to deliver and support the integration of programme and project management.
Portfolio Office	Implementation of roles, process and deliverables standards
	Delivers and supports the integration of programme and project management
	Advice, guidance and support to programmes and projects regarding roles, process and deliverables standards.

Role	Responsibilities
Programme SROs and Project Executives	Confirm understanding and acceptance of roles, process and deliverables standards.
Programme and Project Managers and support	Implementation of, and compliance with, roles, process and deliverables standards.

4.5 STAKEHOLDER ENGAGEMENT AND LEADERSHIP

Good portfolio governance requires good stakeholder engagement – the right people consulted and informed. Stakeholder communications should be an integral part of governance, so that:

- Roles and responsibilities are clearly defined
- Appropriate communications are in place (e.g. monthly reporting on programmes and projects; regular newsletters/bulletins about major initiatives)
- The stakeholders outside the formal Portfolio Organization are engaged and involved.

There are likely to be a number of different, internal stakeholders in the portfolio depending on the nature of the organization. The expectations, needs and interests of each of the stakeholder groups will need to be well understood and managed. Table 4.2 highlights stakeholders and an indication of their likely delivery role(s). The exact titles of the roles will vary from organization to organization. An individual might have more than one role; they are not mutually exclusive.

Table 4.2 Stakeholder Engagement and Leadership

Who	Perspective	Responsibilities
Organization's senior management	Stewardship	Accountable for the organization's performance and delivery of strategic objectives.
Portfolio Board members	Setting strategic direction	Making informed decisions on all or a subset (typically mission critical) of the programmes and projects in the portfolio, e.g. go ahead, stop, defer, re-scope or re-assign resources.
Investment decision-making function (e.g. investment board)	Corporate overview of investments	Making informed investment decisions about proposals set out in business cases (on the basis of benefit to the organization, cost and risk), and possible advice from the Portfolio Office.
Portfolio Office	Corporate overview of current delivery portfolio Centre of change excellence	Creating the programme/project register and managing the agreed portfolio on behalf of the management board (or investment board). Providing dashboard information upon which informed decisions can be made by the management board. Home for portfolio standards and governance.
Programme and project owners Their senior supplier equivalents	Individual programmes and projects	Ensuring successful delivery of outcomes through programmes and projects.
Programme and Project Managers	Individual programmes and projects	Managing the delivery of programmes and projects, providing the Portfolio Office with progress reports and responding to standards required by the Portfolio Office.

Table 4.2 Stakeholder Engagement and Leadership – *continued*

Who	Perspective	Responsibilities
Operational business owners Their senior supplier equivalents	Ongoing operational services and benefits realization	Delivering outcomes through operational services.
Business Change Managers and Change Managers	Benefits realization	Driving benefits realization.

4.5.1 Roles and responsibilities

The following is a summary of the responsibilities for Stakeholder Engagement within the portfolio:

Role	Responsibilities
Portfolio Board	Contribute requirements to the content and process of Stakeholder Engagement
	Confirm their understanding and acceptance of the defined stakeholders and the engagement processes
	Report to and are accountable to the organization at board level.
Portfolio Director	Proposes approach to the content and processes of Stakeholder Engagement
	Ensures that Portfolio Board members have a clear understanding of their roles and responsibilities in relation to defined stakeholders and the engagement processes
	Ensures that the Portfolio Office is structured and skilled to deliver and support the content and process of Stakeholder Engagement.
Portfolio Office	Implementation of content and process of Stakeholder Engagement
	Manage process of Stakeholder Engagement
	Advice, guidance and support to programmes and projects in relation to content and process of Stakeholder Engagement.

Role	Responsibilities
Programme SROs and Project Executives	Confirm understanding and acceptance of content and process of Stakeholder Engagement.
Programme and Project Managers and support	Implementation of, and compliance with, content and process of Stakeholder Engagement.

4.6 BENEFITS REALIZATION

The function of the portfolio is to deliver against the Portfolio Strategy. The Portfolio Plan provides the time-based detail of the costs of the programmes and projects, and benefits that will be delivered by them.

4.6.1 Every project must have a Business Case

For the portfolio to have the level of visibility and control that it needs it must have detailed cost and benefit information at the project level. Whilst the benefits of a project may be delivered within or across several tranches of the programme where the project resides, the detail and timing of the costs and benefit realization must be described at the project level. This means that each project must have its own Business Case, and if necessary a Benefits Realization Plan. The value of this is that each project is justified in its own right. This does not mean that each project must be justified in purely financial terms, but in the terms that it puts forward in its Business Case. It may be that an enabling project with high cost and no clear financial benefit is accepted as it allows the delivery of the programme and is therefore critical to the Programme Business Case. A project that will improve customer service in a measurable way may be acceptable, i.e. the cost is justified for the measurable improvement in an aspect of service delivery. It is important that before- and after-measures are taken in the area targeted for improvement, and that any changes are directly attributable to the introduced changes. It is also important to ensure that the targeted area is sufficiently isolated such that other activities and changes do not impact what is to be measured before and after.

Another value of having a Business Case for each project is to ensure business ownership of, buy-in to, and achievability of, the proposed changes. If Business Cases and Benefits Realization Plans are only ever done at the programme level, there is a risk that at the lower level there is a lack of operational commitment to making the changes and realizing the benefits. This understanding and commitment must be formally obtained before the project's Business Case is approved.

Arguing that the delivery of the benefits of a project is done at the programme level and that the programme's Benefits Realization Plan will contain the necessary detail is not acceptable. However, saying that the programme's Benefits Realization Plan does contain the operational commitment to making the changes and realizing the benefits from the project is fine, as long as the:

- Project's Business Case has been signed off by the Project Executive
- Benefit Profiles for the project have been signed off by the operational owners (the people in the operational part of the organization where the project will impact – see below)

- Programme's Benefits Realization Plan contains detail of how the benefits will be achieved in the operational part of the organization where the project will impact, and this is accepted by the project's Change Manager.

The nature and scale of the Business Case that a project would require could be varied according to the profile of the project (e.g. cost, risk, complexity). If this approach were to happen then the type of Business Case that a project with a given profile should require would have to be clearly set out (see Paragraph 4.4.6 'Tailoring the approach to change initiatives of different scale'). Stand-alone projects that are not enabling projects will need their own Benefits Realization Plans.

4.6.2 Benefit Profiles for each Business Case and Benefits Realization Plan

The Business Case for each project should contain Benefit Profiles. These detail the changes that the project will introduce, including timing, scale of benefit etc. The Benefit Profiles are to be signed off by the people in the operational part of the organization where the project will impact – the operational owners. Each Benefit Profile must have one operational owner. An operational owner may own several Benefit Profiles. The aggregate of the benefits in the project's Benefit Profiles must equal the benefits listed in the project's Business Case. How these benefits will be realized must be listed in the Benefits Realization Plan of the programme (or in the Benefits Realization Plans for a stand-alone project). Their relationship is shown in Table 4.3.

4.6.3 Business Case disciplines

Figure 4.16 illustrates some disciplines for making far more likely the successfully delivery of the project against its Business Case.

Table 4.3 Project Benefit Profiles, Business Case and Benefits Realization Plan

Benefit Profiles	Project Business Case	Benefits Realization Plan
Exist for each project	Composed of Benefit Profiles	Should address the realizing of all benefits in the Project Business Case(s)
Should be linked to the deliverables/products in the Project Plan	Value(s) of benefits of Business Case should be matched by aggregate(s) of benefits in Benefit Profiles	Should use Benefit Profiles to state where operational benefits will be realized, when and by whom
Each Benefit Profile must have an Operational Owner	The Business Case cannot be accepted until each Benefit Profile has been signed off by its operational owner	The programme/project cannot proceed unless the Benefits Realization Plan has been signed off by the (Business) Change Manager. The (Business) Change Manager should not sign off the Benefits Realization Plan without confirmation of deliverability of benefits by operational owners of the Benefit Profiles.

Figure 4.16 Project Business Case disciplines

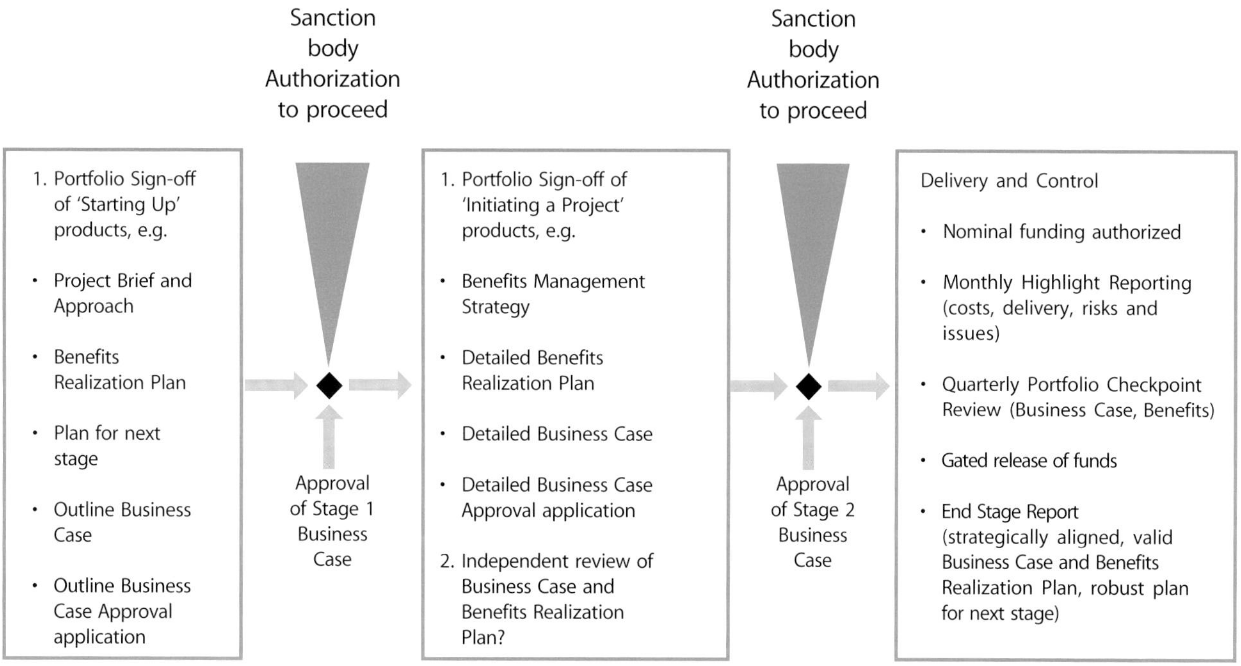

Stepped Business Case approval

If each project is to have a Business Case, there must be a clear process for its approval. A two-stage process, aligned to completion/sign off of the 'Starting Up a Project' and 'Initiating a Project' PRINCE2 stages is shown in Figure 4.16. This ties the Business Case development and approval into the two most appropriate pre-delivery sanctioning points in the PRINCE2 process.

Separation of change governance and financial sanction

The model allows for a separation of approval of:

■ Project deliverables, disciplines and governance (using the project skill-sets of the Portfolio Office)
■ Funding for the next project stage (financial sanction).

In Figure 4.16, the portfolio sign-off of 'Starting Up' products is the application of the change governance sanction and the 'Approval of Stage 1 Business Case' is the application of the financial sanction. Of course, should the project not pass the change governance sanction, there would be no need for the financial sanction. The same approach would apply to the process leading up to the 'Approval of Stage 2 Business Case'.

This accommodates organizations where the portfolio function (home of the change capability, possibly Portfolio Office, Change Board etc.) is separate from the funding approval (finance function, management board), and the portfolio function will (acting in its role of assuring the application of correct project governance and disciplines) advise the funding approver whether or not to sanction funding on to the next stage.

Process disciplines of delivering against the Business Case

Once the Stage 2 Business Case has been approved, there is a series of controls that will apply to the projects in the portfolio.

■ The approved Stage 2 Business Case will have listed the expected lifetime costs and benefits of the project, and authorized this spend against the project plan:
  ● This funding authorization is nominal; there must be appropriate delivery of outputs against plan and to cost for the future release of funds
  ● Gated release of funds with adequate delivery against plan, based on monthly highlight reporting (costs, delivery, risks and issues)
  ● End Stage Report (strategically aligned, valid Business Case and Benefits Realization Plan, robust plan for next stage)
■ Quarterly Portfolio Checkpoint review (project and programme Business Case, Benefits Realization Plans).

Incremental funds release

Incremental funds release is one of the most important controls applied at the project level for ensuring the overall delivery of the portfolio. This means that funding for the next stage of delivery will only be released if a project meets agreed performance criteria. The advantages of this approach are that:

■ Projects are forced to meet their performance criteria (e.g. meeting critical milestones, delivering specific outputs)
■ It provides the leverage to close projects that are not performing
■ It reduces financial risk.

If, for example a programme directly sponsored by the organization's CEO should be stopped, it is the responsibility of the Portfolio Director and Programme SRO to convince the CEO of the necessity to halt funding for the project's next stage.

There are several models for incremental funding, which include:

- Releasing only a small percentage of the required funding at the start of the project
- Ring-fencing the project budget (and apply stage-gating for release – see above)
- Putting funding for cross-cutting projects into a central budget.

4.6.4 Role of the Portfolio Office in benefits assurance

In a portfolio environment, the Portfolio Office plays a critical role in assuring that the delivery of benefits of the portfolio are planned, realistic and are actually delivered. This goes down to the level of:

- Programme and Project Business Case approval (including objectives, scope, sponsorship, ROI, alignment to strategic objectives, dependencies)
- Ensuring Project Business Cases are valid
- Making sure that realization of benefits is owned by the relevant business area(s) of the organization.

Whilst the Portfolio Board selects the programmes and projects for inclusion in the portfolio, this is likely to be with advice from the Portfolio Director, who will be supported by the Portfolio Office. Subsequently the Portfolio Office should collate the reports on progress against plans, so that the Portfolio Board can make informed decisions about the portfolio.

The Portfolio Office should support the Portfolio Board in selecting programmes and projects:

1 Investigate the business cases for individual programmes and projects:

- Is it worth doing? Determine the contribution to strategic objectives, benefits, added value
- Is it achievable and do stakeholders support it?

2 Check the programme/project's fit within the portfolio and corporate priorities:

- Even though it is worth doing, there may be higher priorities.

3 Confirm that the programme or project should go ahead:

- Ensure that the delivery approach has been thought through and that the team's competencies match the initiative.

4 Revisit individual programmes and projects at decision points (end of stage, agreed health-check, formal review point etc.):

- Has the strategy changed? Are priorities different? Are resources no longer available?
- What should be done if a project is out of control?
- What would be the impact of redeploying resources to support failing projects?
- These reviews should be planned, agreed events, rather than anything ad-hoc or informal.

5 How will the programme project be segmented?

- How will it get the right business ownership and commitment?

6 Are there dependencies to be managed?

- What impact might it have on other programmes and projects in the portfolio?

The Portfolio Office should also support the Portfolio Board in benefits tracking and ongoing management of the portfolio:

- Track the portfolio's performance and progress against outcomes
- Take prompt corrective action when required
- Support the making of hard choices when needed – provide the analysis and recommendations for the Portfolio Board to reprioritize, defer or stop projects
- Check monthly on the mission-critical projects
- Monitor the organization's total exposure to risk
- Look to the future – plan for known changes and forecast the future demands on resources.

Underpinning the above activities, the Portfolio Office has two main roles:

- Supporting the delivery against the Portfolio Control Framework
- Ensuring the programmes and projects of the portfolio adopt and abide by the Change Delivery Framework.

All the other tasks that the Portfolio Office may undertake will be derived form these two main responsibilities.

4.6.5 Roles and responsibilities

The following is a summary of the responsibilities for the embedding and management of effective benefits realization within the portfolio:

Role	Responsibilities
Portfolio Board	Contribute requirements to the content and process of benefits realization
	Confirm their understanding and acceptance of their roles and responsibilities in relation to the content and process of benefits realization.
Portfolio Director	Proposes approach to the content and process of benefits realization
	Ensures that Portfolio Board members have a clear understanding of their roles and responsibilities in relation to the content and process of benefits realization
	Ensures that the Portfolio Office is structured and skilled to deliver and support the content and process of benefits realization.
Portfolio Office	Implementation of the content and process of benefits realization
	Manage process of benefits realization
	Advice, guidance and support to programmes and projects in relation to content and process of benefits realization.
Programme SROs and Project Executives	Confirm their understanding and acceptance of their roles and responsibilities in relation to the content and process of benefits realization.
Programme and Project Managers and support	Implementation of, and compliance with, content and process of benefits realization.

4.7 PORTFOLIO PLANNING AND CONTROL

Portfolio planning and management processes underpin the governance framework. Planning and control are necessary for the success of any portfolio and should be seen as distinctly separate concepts and activities.

4.7.1 Portfolio planning

As stated before, the planning activities should be aligned with corporate business planning and spending rounds. Some organizations are able to plan as much as ten years in advance; for others it may not be possible to plan with confidence more than three to five years ahead.

Scenario planning is a useful technique for dealing with uncertainty in planning. It allows for examination of different combinations of programmes and projects, using what-if questions about different timeframes, resource profiles and so on.

Portfolio Plan

As discussed earlier, the preparation of the Portfolio Plan involves:

- Processing large amounts of information
- Extensive consultation
- Building the plan.

During its early iterations the Portfolio Plan will include many unknowns and a high level of ambiguity.

The Portfolio Plan is not something that is created and then left untouched. It is a document (providing control via the gates and control points inside it, showing what will be achieved by when and the interdependencies between projects, programmes etc.) for the portfolio. It forms a complete picture of how the portfolio is going to work. When constituent programme and project plans are developed, they will be aligned to, and in part embedded in, the Portfolio Plan. It enables the Portfolio Director, on behalf of the Portfolio Board, to implement a planned and controlled environment that can be monitored and maintained throughout the life of the portfolio.

The Portfolio Plan should include the following core information:

- Programme and project timescales, costs, outputs and dependencies (these will be taken out to be managed via the portfolio and programme scheduling and budgeting systems and processes)
- Risks and assumptions (for taking and managing via the portfolio risks and issues logs)
- Schedule showing the portfolio's expected performance at main review points (derived from the programme tranches and delivery schedules of the stand-alone projects) – each programme and project should have standard milestones and transition gates used to review progress at portfolio level
- Benefits delivery schedule (derived from the Benefits Realization Plans of the programmes and stand-alone projects of the portfolio)
- Transition plans
- Monitoring and control activities and performance targets.

Developing the Portfolio Plan requires an understanding of the:

- Validity, strategic alignment and priority implicit in the Portfolio Strategy
- Composition of the portfolio, as given in the Portfolio Schedule
- Requirements with respect to prioritization, categorization and segmentation, as drafted in the Portfolio Strategy
- Level of detail in the Portfolio Plan needed to:
  - Provide adequate information about progress to enable decision making
  - Identify critical dependencies and other issues that may affect progress

- Information to be used to monitor and maintain the Portfolio Plan, including how:
  - Information from the Portfolio Plan will be presented to stakeholders
  - Information from the Portfolio Plan will be distributed, to whom, and when
  - Programme and stand-alone project-level information will be integrated at the portfolio level.

Alongside this is the need to ensure the ongoing triangular alignment of the Portfolio Strategy, Portfolio Plan and Portfolio Schedule, to confirm:

- Ongoing alignment of the portfolio with corporate objectives and goals (Portfolio Strategy)
- Detailed, owned programmes and projects operating within defined control and constraints (Portfolio Schedule)
- Clear strategic delivery, spend and benefit realization milestones (Portfolio Plan).

Whilst Benefit Profiles and Benefits Realization Plans are often initially developed separately from the Portfolio Plan, collaboration between these activities is critical. The total set of Benefit Profiles, together with the Benefits Realization Plans, need to be integrated with the Portfolio Plan to ensure the dependencies on project delivery and transition are properly considered (and made central to the risk management activities).

Developing and maintaining the Portfolio Plan requires the aggregation of all the Programme and Project Plans. The focus for portfolio planning is on the interdependencies between the programmes and projects and any dependencies on external factors outside the control of the portfolio. This makes portfolio planning and monitoring a complex task.

The portfolio's journey is ongoing, reflecting the portfolio's business-as-usual role. Hence, early portfolio designs (or designs made early in the planning cycle of the portfolio)

may well have very little detail of new programmes and projects, and estimates for the duration and cost of these may be based on huge assumptions.

Scheduling

Constructing the schedule of programme and project delivery demonstrates realization of benefits aligned with the strategic objectives that set the context for the portfolio. In order to achieve this, the Portfolio Plan needs to:

- Integrate the increasing refinement of individual programme and stand-alone project plans (as each proceeds through its lifecycle into the Portfolio Plan to inform and assess progress)
- Respond to programme exception situations that mean a reassessment of the Portfolio Plan
- Continually monitor and review progress against the Portfolio Plan (and Portfolio Strategy), including looking forward to anticipate emerging risks to the Portfolio Plan.

Scheduling staff require better estimation skills than most organizations have, and the portfolio will need to recognize this if the Portfolio Plan is to have adequate validity. The Portfolio Plan's schedule provides the overall sequence and timetable for the portfolio by incorporating the dependency network and the timescales for each of the programmes (and their projects).

Prioritization

The defined priorities influence portfolio scheduling. The effect on staff and the rest of the portfolio of delaying or bringing forward a particular programme can be significant. The prioritization of the portfolio (as reflected in the Portfolio Plan) should acknowledge critical portfolio constraints and requirements, for example:

- Specific programmes/projects, such as procurements, whose outcomes/outputs are prerequisites for other, future programmes or projects
- Resource requirements, such as specific skills that may be scarce
- Early benefits realization, such as reduced operational costs, that will help engender continued commitment and enthusiasm for the portfolio.

Resources

Any input required by a project or programme is a resource. The term covers people, assets, materials, funding and services. Shared resources (those resources that will be used by two or more projects or programmes) should be planned and managed by the portfolio. Developing the Portfolio Plan will identify those resources that need to be shared between programmes and projects. Minimizing resource sharing between programmes and projects will help prevent bottlenecks occurring. Against that, maximizing resource sharing will help promote knowledge sharing and organizational learning.

Many resources have both operational and portfolio obligations. The acquisition of such resources needs careful consideration, in particular how conflicts will be resolved when a resource is required in more than one place at the same time. Preparing in advance for such problems will make it easier to prioritize when necessary. It should also be borne in mind that people resources are more effective when dedicated to a particular project rather than being expected to multi-task.

It is important to remember that resources (especially people) have finite availability, skills and experience. The combination of these factors is their capability to contribute to the changes required. This will determine the maximum pace at which work can progress. The portfolio must ensure that setting expectations and planning at all levels does not disregard the limits of capability, otherwise unrealistic plans may be developed. Of all the resources that a portfolio will consume, it is often availability of capability that will present the most compelling constraint.

The Portfolio Plan should include resource schedules (derived from the Resource Management Strategies of the programmes) describing how resources will be identified, acquired, and managed. It should also provide rules and direction on how to resolve resource problems.

Resource management plans

A major part of portfolio planning is to consider what resources the portfolio will require, and how they will be acquired, used, shared and managed effectively. How this will be approached is defined in the resource management plans that form part of the Portfolio Plan. Portfolio resources will include the:

- Portfolio's financial needs as expressed in the Portfolio Strategy, together with the detail and aggregation of programme and project budgets and expenditure profiles, and the portfolio accounting procedures
- Staff and other personnel involved in the portfolio, and its programmes and projects. This should include those who will be affected by its outcome(s) even if their involvement may be minimal (as they will need to be available at the right time to change to the new way of working)
- Assets the programmes and projects of the portfolio will use, e.g. buildings and equipment
- Systems, services and technology the programmes and projects of the portfolio will use as part of their delivery.

Resource sharing

Shared resources represent a set of dependencies between the programmes and projects of the portfolio and therefore need to be managed effectively and used efficiently. Scarcity of shared resources often creates more critical constraints on the progress of the programmes and projects of the portfolio than even the logical dependencies between project outputs.

The resource management plans developed as part of the Portfolio Plan is to ensure the resources required match the planned activities and timescales. The Portfolio Plan also implements the resource management plans, reflecting the timeline for the requirement of the resources, when and who will be implementing them.

It is increasingly common practice to resolve the inevitable work peaks created during the development of a portfolio by applying a resource levelling model which uses external associates or outsourcing to overcome resource bottlenecks and scarcity.

Portfolio Schedule

The Portfolio Schedule contains a summary description of all the programmes and projects that together, through their combined outcomes and outputs, will deliver the Portfolio Strategy. The Portfolio Schedule should include the following information about each programme and project:

- High-level statement of what the programme/project will deliver
- Description of the programme outcomes and project outputs, including the contribution it will make to benefits realization
- Programme/project name
- Which parts of the organization the programme/project will impact
- Expected costs
- Delivery timelines (i.e. what, when)

- Segmentation of the programme/project (i.e. in which portfolio/sub-portfolio/programme; confirming the part of the organization where the programme/project will be owned)
- Expected owner of the programme/project
- Categorization of the programme/project
- Priority of the programme/project
- Dependencies with other projects
- Risk-related information, the risk profile for each particular programme and project, as well as the contribution of each project to the overall risk profile of the portfolio.

These should mirror the content of the Programme Briefs and Project Briefs (for stand-alone projects) that will be developed by the portfolio to give each programme and project a thorough and rapid start.

One of the objectives for designing the portfolio is to place clear and direct accountability on the programmes and projects, while avoiding a spaghetti-like tangle of interdependencies. This can be achieved by ensuring that the delineation of programme and project boundaries maximizes the internal consistency of the programmes and projects, acting to minimize the number of interfaces and dependencies both between the projects and across programmes.

4.7.2 Portfolio control

Portfolio control provides supporting activities and processes to the standards that will be applied in:

- Ensuring clear visibility and control of budgets, milestones, dependencies
- Resourcing planning, review and allocation
- Reporting and decision making (to include resolving redundancies and overlaps across projects)
- Forecasting, and acting on this to:
  - Refine and improve delivery

- Minimize the impact of ambiguity and
- Bring certainty wherever possible.

Managing the portfolio does not mean micro-management of the programmes and projects within it. Communicating the right information between the portfolio and its programmes and projects is a major consideration when establishing portfolio controls. Programmes and projects should be empowered but need clear tolerances and limits to ensure they do not exceed their delegated authority. Allowing the programme and project managers to manage their programmes and projects within the tolerances set by the portfolio is an essential part of good portfolio management.

The aim of the portfolio is, through the achievement of the aggregation of desired programme outcomes (and the realization of their expected benefits), to meet the goals and targets of the Portfolio Strategy. One of the greatest challenges in running a portfolio is to reconcile programme and project objectives and accountability with overall portfolio goals and portfolio-level consistency and control. Factors such as programme and project management experience, portfolio risk and available margins should all be assessed when determining how tightly the portfolio controls its programmes and projects. All of these factors should be reflected in the individual programmes' Monitoring and Control Strategies (which set out the approach the individual programmes will take to applying these internal controls). The portfolio will need to set out its monitoring and control requirements, so that these may be embedded in the controls and processed at programme and project level.

The communication flow between the portfolio and its programmes and projects should aim to reuse information contained in standards introduced as part of the portfolio governance. Programme and project documents (Blueprints, PIDs etc.), highlight reports, exception reports, Issue and Risk Registers will provide much of the information required by the portfolio. Part of the role of the Portfolio Office is to support this reporting.

Performance reporting of the programmes and projects

Effective portfolio decisions are based on the accurate measurement of data and the analysis of reliable information. This is as true for the portfolio as it is for any part of an organization. For the portfolio (or the programmes and projects within it) to be able to measure progress and assess performance, measures of inputs, resources, activities and outputs will need to be taken prior to any change throughout the programmes and projects of the portfolio. The data and information from these measures will need to be analysed and reviewed at the regular meetings set out in the portfolio's quality schedule (in part aggregated from the programmes' quality schedules). This approach will enable the portfolio to be more flexible to changes in the business environment and prevent fire-fighting. This is because the portfolio's leaders will be responding to hard facts and figures, and relying less on intuition.

Portfolio measurement and review

Measurements across a portfolio can be considered in three main ways:

- Those concerned with the management and control of the programmes and projects, for example cost and budget reports
- The measurement of the portfolio's performance to assess if acceptable benefits are materializing
- Reviewing priorities and resource allocation within the portfolio, relative to the (possibly changing) strategic priorities of the organization.

Unsuitable measures or misinterpreted analysis are likely to lead to poor control. Quality control should ensure measurement and analysis procedures and systems are effective.

Frequency of reporting and review

Within programmes, and more particularly projects, review points may sometimes be built around deliverables. This means that performance reviews may not take place in a regular and recurrent manner. This would not work in a portfolio environment. Effective portfolio control is built on standardization and regularity of reporting. Below is a tried and well-proven reporting timeline:

1 Projects' work-streams should report to the project on a weekly basis

2 The projects should report to the programme on a weekly basis with updates, and on a monthly basis with a more detailed performance update

3 The programmes should report performance to the portfolio on a monthly basis.

4 The portfolio should review its performance and that of the programmes relative to the organization's strategy on a quarterly basis – this is the time for ensuring alignment of the portfolio (and reprioritization of the programmes and projects)

5 The Portfolio Strategy, together with categorization, prioritization and future-looking balance of the portfolio, should be reviewed on an at-least annual basis.

Reporting content

The suggested content of the various recurrent reports is summarized in Table 4.4.

Programme and Project Boards

For the monthly and quarterly review and control cycles to work, the timing of the Programme and Project Board meetings may need to be formalized to happen on a monthly basis, with for example:

- Week 1
  Project Board meetings to take place
  Project Boards confirm their project's monthly report

- Week 2
  Programme Board meetings to take place
  Programme Boards ratify (or request further information on) the projects' reporting
  Programme Boards confirm their programme's monthly reporting

- Week 3
  Portfolio team ratifies (or requests further information on) the programmes' reporting
  Portfolio team reports portfolio performance, with highlights and issues, to the Portfolio Director

- Week 4
  Portfolio team requests further information and clarification of issues of the programme and projects
  Portfolio team seeks confirmation from stakeholders to outstanding issues, and model alternate scenarios/solutions.

Table 4.4 Suggested reporting content

Reporting element	Content
Work-stream reporting – weekly	Progress against work-stream milestones
	Issues that need addressing.
Project reporting – weekly	Progress against project milestones
	Issues that need addressing.
Project reporting – monthly	Progress against project milestones, deliverables and/or products
	Issues that need addressing
	Updated Risk Register and Issue Log
	Update on project dependencies (both ways)
	Position in project lifecycle
	RAG (Red Amber Green) status
	Anticipated RAG status at the next reporting date (this is an effective way to show management that the team are identifying future improvements enabling a move from, say, Amber to Green or challenges to the project with a possible likely movement from, say, Amber to Red)
	Financial performance in year and over project lifecycle
	Deliverability of benefits
	Actual and expected resource usage
	Outcomes of any audits, reviews or health-checks.
	continued overleaf

Table 4.4 Suggested reporting content – *continued*

Reporting element	Content
Programme reporting – monthly	Progress against programme milestones
	Issues raised from projects that need addressing at programme level
	Updated Programme Risk Register and Issue Log
	Update on any programme dependencies (both ways)
	RAG (Red Amber Green) status
	Anticipated RAG status at the next reporting date
	Financial performance in year and over project lifecycle
	Actual and expected deliverability of benefits, with respect to the Programme Business Case
	Actual and expected programme resource usage
	Outcomes of any audits, reviews or health-checks.
Programme reporting – quarterly	Progress against programme milestones
	Issues raised from projects that need addressing at programme level
	Updated Programme Risk Register and Issue Log
	Update on any programme dependencies (both ways)
	RAG (Red Amber Green) status
	Financial performance in year and over project lifecycle
	Actual and expected deliverability of benefits with respect to the Programme Business Case
	Actual and expected programme resource usage
	Outcome of any audits, reviews or health-checks
	Priority level (e.g. mission critical, highly desirable)
	Confirmation of people in roles
	Summary/overall risk score
	Actual and expected performance against Portfolio Strategy
	Organization's strategies/targets that programme delivers against
	Impact of not delivering the programme.

Table 4.4 Suggested reporting content – *continued*

Reporting element	Content
Portfolio reporting – quarterly	Progress against milestones in Portfolio Strategy
	Issues raised from programme that need addressing at portfolio level
	Portfolio-level issues that need addressing
	Updated Portfolio (corporate?) Risk Register and Issue Log
	Portfolio financial performance in year and projected over next year(s)
	Actual and expected delivery of change and benefits with respect to the Portfolio Strategy
	Actual and expected portfolio resource usage
	Summary view of outcomes of any audits, reviews or health-checks, and recommendations
	Confirm upcoming schedule of any audits, reviews or health-checks
	Confirm which projects are in which defined portfolio categories
	Confirmation of any changes of people in roles
	Actual and expected performance against Portfolio Strategy
	Any proposed changes to portfolio balance (new and completed/closed programmes and projects)
	How portfolio will look after proposed changes to portfolio
	Confirmation of alignment of programmes in proposed portfolio to organization's strategies/targets.

continued overleaf

Table 4.4 Suggested reporting content – *continued*

Reporting element	Content
Portfolio reporting – annually	Portfolio performance:
	Progress against milestones in Portfolio Strategy
	Issues raised from programme that need addressing at portfolio level
	Portfolio-level issues that need addressing
	Updated Portfolio (corporate?) Risk Register and Issue Log
	Portfolio financial performance for year and projected over next year(s)
	Actual delivery of change and benefits with respect to the Portfolio Strategy
	Actual portfolio resource usage
	Summary view of outcomes of any audits, reviews or health-checks, and recommendations
	Confirmation of upcoming schedule of any audits, reviews or health-checks.
	Portfolio alignment:
	Statement of revised Portfolio Strategy (a re-statement of current Portfolio Strategy is not acceptable)
	Statement of (revised) portfolio categories
	Confirm which projects are in which defined portfolio categories
	Revised programme and project prioritization across and within categories
	Profile of expected portfolio resource usage
	Statement of expected performance against Portfolio Strategy (including alignment of programmes in proposed portfolio to organization's strategies/targets)
	Aggregate risk profile for revised portfolio balance
	Confirmation of any changes of people/new people in roles.

4.7.3 Roles and responsibilities

The following is a summary of the responsibilities for effective planning and control within the portfolio:

Role	Responsibilities
Portfolio Board	Contribute requirements to the content and processes of planning and control
	Confirm their understanding and acceptance of their roles and responsibilities in relation to the content and processes of planning and control.
Portfolio Director	Proposes approach to the content and processes of planning and control
	Ensures that Portfolio Board members have a clear understanding of their roles and responsibilities in relation to the content and processes of planning and control
	Ensures the Portfolio Office is structured and skilled to deliver and support the content and processes of planning and control.
Portfolio Office	Implements the content and process of planning and control
	Manages process of planning and control
	Gives advice, guidance and support to programmes and projects in relation to content and processes of planning and control.
Programme SROs and Project Executives	Confirm their understanding and acceptance of their roles and responsibilities in relation to content and processes of planning and control.
Programme and Project Managers and support	Implementation of, and compliance with, content and processes of planning and control.

4.8 RISK MANAGEMENT

Implementing the Portfolio Plan will inevitably have risks associated with it. Individual projects may face critical risks that, should they materialize, could affect the entire portfolio. All assumptions should be regarded and managed as risks. The identification of these, together with suitable responses, should be part of the portfolio's risk management activities. Such activities and contingency for risk should be included in the Portfolio Plan, based on a defined Risk Management Strategy. The Risk Management Strategy should define the procedures and process for escalating risks and issues from project to programme to the portfolio. The numbering convention for risk and issues should allow for easily identifying the segmented derivation of the risk or issue (i.e. relevant programme or project). The Risk Register should ensure that all risks have a common proximity/criticality/business-impact identification process and that individual risks can be assigned and reported at project, programme and portfolio level.

4.8.1 Risk and return

There needs to be agreement at the Portfolio Board about the organization's willingness to take on risk and thus define its risk appetite. The demands of the Portfolio Strategy will predicate the level of change to the organization; and the level of change that the organization must embrace will to a large part determine the aggregate level of risk within the portfolio.

However, within this, the level of risk and the expected return (measurable beneficial change) of each programme may vary wildly. At the portfolio level there will need to be complete clarity about the risks – the interdependencies and constraints as well as the individual risks in aggregate.

The levels of balance of risk and return that each programme presents will be important selection criteria. The aim is to achieve (at the portfolio level also) the appropriate balance of achievability (in relation to risk) and value (in terms of return for the investment – not just in cash terms, but economic value in terms of policy outcomes).

It is therefore important to consider risk from several perspectives:

- The impact of risks associated with a particular programme activity on the business
- The impact of the aggregated risk (or all of the portfolio activity) on the business
- How risk can be reduced by selecting the right programmes and projects
- How benefits realization can be optimized by effective management of risks
- How prioritization and scheduling of the programmes and projects may affect the risk profile.

Value in the context of risk and return

Value should always be assessed as the whole-life value – that is, the benefits that will accrue to the organization over the life of the investment. For example, a building might have an operational life of a hundred years or so, but is only useful to the organization for the next ten years in helping to deliver benefits in the shape of improved services. This is an essential principle of investment appraisal and is much more important as a deciding factor than aspects such as NPV, ROI and cost avoidance. Other considerations include:

- The benefits to be achieved by other parties in the value chain
- The financial aspects such as profit and loss and cash flow.

4.8.2 Risk and prioritization

It is often the case that a new, high-priority major project (strategically important and/or major business or technical change issues, and/or requiring significant delivery capability) is inherently of high risk (where there is radical change, complexity or innovation, uncertainty of outcome, large scale, and sensitivity if the project fails or multiple partners/delivery agents are involved).

Therefore if the portfolio is to deliver according to the needs of the Portfolio Strategy, the approach taken for each of the projects must de-risk the project, in accordance with the priority of the project. Normally de-risking a project will result in changes to the Project Approach, and will have an impact on dimension such as cost, time, level of benefits to be delivered etc.

4.8.3 Countering major programme risk factors

Many programmes will feature more than one category of risk, so the options for reducing the risks may need to be a combination of several approaches.

Some examples of high-risk elements on programmes and possible approaches to mitigate these, is shown below:

- **'Big bang' implementation** – one or more of the following: no way back to a more stable environment; all or most of the requirements/functions/functionality are delivered in one single step; the programme is delivered to all or most of the customers in one step; all or most of the benefits of the investment in business change are dependent on completion of the programme, with no significant benefits delivered
  - Possible mitigations: Adopt a phased implementation or pilot the new environment; look to break the delivery into distinct, separate units, each with its own associated benefits

- **Complexity** – a number of complex elements, high degree of interdependency with other programmes and/or technology innovation
  - Possible mitigations: make dependency management one of the main elements of the approach to delivery of the programmes, reduce dependency by taking dependency into the programme (i.e. risk reduction via inclusion), seek to reduce the complexity by breaking delivery down into smaller, less complex units

- **Uncertainty** – about whether the proposed solution to a problem will work and/or where the requirement is unclear and/or the end-user needs will be met
  - Possible mitigations: Put greater emphasis on user involvement and user buy-in/ownership; conduct review of solution acceptability to the users; formally review and re-accept the user requirements; trial or pilot the solution

- **Scale** – large numbers of people involved and/or multiple customer groups and/or wide geographical spread affected by the programme
  - Possible mitigations: Segment the programme in smaller units that are more controllable; if feasible, look to localize ownership and delivery; reduce number of people involved by having formal lead users etc. with appropriate governance and communication to ensure their ownership is valid and truly representative

- **Sensitivity** – likelihood of embarrassment for the department if the programme fails
  - Possible mitigations: ensure programmes have necessary levels of senior-level commitment and resources; look to reduce risk via phasing, piloting etc.

- **Multiple partners/delivery agents** – e.g. cross-cutting/joined-up implementation
- Possible mitigations: look to reduce (transfer) risk by appointing lead partners/delivery agents; look to implement risk/reward sharing with payments to all partners/delivery agents depending on final outcomes and overall successful delivery.

4.8.4 Portfolio Risk Management Strategy

Before embarking on any risk management activities, a Risk Management Strategy should be developed for the portfolio. The purpose of this strategy is to describe the specific risk management activities that will be undertaken to support effective risk management within the portfolio. The strategy will typically include those described next.

Introduction
States the purpose and owner of the strategy.

Outline of the portfolio
Provides a summary of the portfolio (e.g. goals and risk appetite as identified by the Portfolio Strategy, scope of the portfolio and level of defined portfolio-level and individual, programme-specific risk, and any specific areas of risk or focus identified in the Portfolio Plan).

Roles and responsibilities
Describes the main roles and responsibilities within the portfolio.

Risk management process
How the portfolio will manage the process of identifying, assessing and mitigating risks, to be adapted depending on the nature of the portfolio.

Scales for estimating probability and impact

These should be developed for each programme in the portfolio to ensure that the scales for cost and time (for instance) are relevant to the cost and timeframe of the programme. These may be shown in the form of probability impact grids giving the criteria for each level within the scale, e.g. for very high, high, medium, low and very low.

Expected values

Provides guidance on calculating expected value, which is done by multiplying the average impact by the probability percentage. By totalling the expected values for all the risks associated with a programme, an understanding of the risk exposure faced by the programmes, and total risk exposure faced by the portfolio, can be calculated.

Proximity

Provides guidance on how this time factor for risks is to be assessed. Proximity reflects the fact that risks will occur at particular times and the severity of their impact will vary according to when they occur.

Risk response category

The responses available will depend on whether the risk is a perceived threat or an opportunity. Table 4.5 describes the alternative responses for a threat and Table 4.6 describes those for an opportunity.

Budget required

Describes the budget required to support risk management throughout the planning cycle of the portfolio, and the life of the programmes.

Tools and techniques

Refers to any preferred techniques to be used for each step of the process described above.

Templates

These might include a Risk Register.

Early-warning indicators

These will be selected for their relevance to the programmes with portfolio, and for the portfolio as a whole.

Timing of risk management activities

Will state when formal risk management activities are to be undertaken (e.g. as part of end-of-tranche reviews for the programmes, and to tie with the periodic portfolio reviews).

Reporting

Describes the reports that are to be produced and records their purpose, timing and recipients.

4.8.5 Treating risks as threats and opportunities

Treating risks as threats

Using M_o_R terminology, Table 4.5 shows the categories under which the risks may be treated as threats when being addressed.

Treating risks as opportunities

Using M_o_R terminology Table 4.6 shows the categories under which the risks may be treated as opportunities when being addressed.

Table 4.5 Threat responses for risks

Reduction	Proactive actions taken to reduce: the probability of the event occurring, by performing some form of control the impact of the event should it occur.
Removal	Typically involves changing some aspect of the programme, e.g. changing the scope, procurement route, supplier or sequence of activities.
Transfer	A third party takes on responsibility for an aspect of the threat, e.g. for example through insurance or by means of appropriate clauses in a contract.
Retention	A conscious and deliberate decision is taken to retain the threat, having discerned that it is more economical to do so than to attempt a risk response action, for example. The threat should continue to be monitored to ensure that it remains tolerable.
Share	Modern procurement methods commonly entail a form of risk sharing through the application of a pain/gain formula: both parties share the gain (within pre-agreed limits) if the cost is less than the cost plan; or share the pain (again within pre-agreed limits) if the cost plan is exceeded. Several industries include risk-sharing principles within their contracts with third parties.

Table 4.6 Opportunity responses for risks

Realization	Identifying and seizing an opportunity: The realization of an opportunity ensures that potential improvements to the programme are delivered. For example, if there is an opportunity to complete a project early and reduce the headcount, the realization of the opportunity would be to achieve the reduced costs possible through a lower-than-planned headcount.
Enhancement	Seizing and improving on an identified opportunity: Enhancement of an opportunity refers to both the realization of an opportunity and achieving additional gains over and above the opportunity. An example may be negotiating a lower rental figure for existing occupied premises and restructuring the organization to reduce the floor space required. Or it may include achieving financial gain from finishing a project early and gaining additional revenue from deploying the released resources on another programme or project.
Exploitation	Identifying and seizing multiple benefits: Exploitation refers to changing (a programme's?) scope, supplier or specification to achieve a beneficial outcome without changing the objectives or specification. An example is where a contractor on a fixed-price contract manages to obtain a lower price from an alternative supplier on multiple subcontracts, while maintaining the desired specification.

4.8.6 Roles and responsibilities

The following is a summary of the responsibilities for the embedding and management of effective risk management within the portfolio:

Role	Responsibilities
Portfolio Board	Contribute requirements to the content and process of risk management
	Confirm their understanding and acceptance of their roles and responsibilities in relation to the content and process of risk management.
Portfolio Director	Proposes approach to the content and process of risk management
	Ensures that Portfolio Board members have a clear understanding of their roles and responsibilities in relation to the content and process of risk management
	Ensures that the Portfolio Office is structured and skilled to deliver and support the content and process of risk management.
Portfolio Office	Implementation of the content and process of risk management
	Manages process of risk management
	Advice, guidance and support to programmes and projects in relation to content and process of risk management.
Programme SROs and Project Executives	Confirm their understanding and acceptance of their roles and responsibilities in relation to the content and process of risk management.
Programme and Project Managers and support	Implementation of, and compliance with, content and process of risk management.

It is likely that an organization that can afford all these roles would probably have its own risk management function. In such a case the risk management function would likely take on defining the corporate risk management approach within which the management of portfolio risk would take place.

Portfolio Office

Annex A: Portfolio Office

The Portfolio Office is the focal point for portfolio management activities. It should be seen by the programmes as the hub for:

- Setting and policing standards
- Collecting progress reports from the programmes and their constituent projects
- Performance review and recommendation on portfolio changes
- Planning and coordinating the allocation of resources across programmes.

There are roles that the Portfolio Office should perform.

A.1   SUPPORTING THE PORTFOLIO DIRECTOR

The Portfolio Director will need a support team (see Figure A.1). Unlike programme and project support with its focus on programme and project delivery, this team is focused on monitoring and assuring performance across the portfolio, against the criteria set out in the Portfolio Strategy. The areas of activity covered by the Portfolio Office would include:

- Ensuring portfolio adherence to the organization's extra-portfolio strategies, policies and standards
- Establishing quality processes
- Establishing and running the portfolio's configuration management standards
- Programme and project audits and health-checks

Figure A.1 Supporting the Portfolio Director

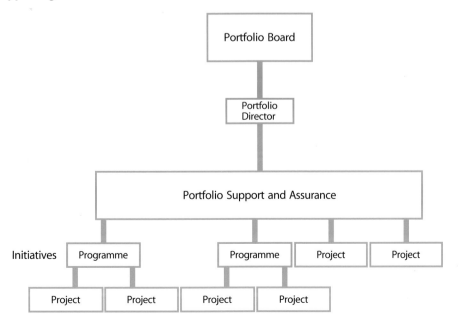

- Control of procurement, partners and suppliers
- Providing a centre of excellence and best practice for the portfolio change standards
- Embedding the portfolio change standards (i.e. how the portfolio and the programmes and projects within it will operate)
- Supporting the programmes and projects and their Programme/Project Offices in adoption of, and adherence to, the portfolio change standards
- Defining and running the performance reporting of the programmes and projects
- Supporting the Portfolio Director in his accountability and reporting to the enterprise-level board
- Performing those activities that would be performed by comparable central change support functions, such as corporate programme office, central portfolio office, group change governance etc.

A.2 ADHERENCE TO STRATEGIES, POLICIES AND STANDARDS

The portfolio should be driven by the organization's policies and strategies. Quality activities in a portfolio need to ensure that the planned changes continue to be correctly aligned to the relevant parts of these corporate strategies and policies. Also, organizations review and change their policies and strategies at intervals that are unlikely to coincide with a convenient portfolio review point. A monitoring and informing mechanism to alert the portfolio team of pending policy or strategy changes will help in two ways:

- The portfolio team can provide input to the policy and strategy makers, to explain how well it is progressing in line with current policy and strategy. This may help strategy makers avoid changing direction because, for example, they have not seen evidence that current strategy is working.

- It enables the portfolio team to assess the impact of proposals to change policy and strategy. What might be gained and what will be lost can be fed back to the strategist or policy maker, so their decisions are made on a more informed basis.

Many organizations have a quality management system that supports operations to ensure their products and services satisfactorily meet their customers' requirements. Where such a system exists the portfolio team needs to be aware of how quality standards relate to planned changes in the portfolio. New improved operations may still need to comply with these standards, or the quality standards may need to be adjusted to suit the amended process, products or services.

There are few business activities that are not subject to some aspect of legislation and or regulation. The portfolio needs to be aware which laws and regulations are relevant to ensure its programmes' outcomes, projects' outputs and the changed operations comply correctly. Similar to the reasons explained above for policy and strategy, portfolio teams need to monitor these external standards to detect and assess the impact of any pending changes. This point is also important in the context of technical or professional standards. For example, if an organization advertises itself as complying with ISO 9000, then it must ensure it can still comply after changes have been embedded.

A.3 ESTABLISHING QUALITY PROCESSES

A process is a set of related activities that are carried out in a defined order. A system contains several processes and requires good management infrastructure and control mechanisms for all of its parts to work together properly. The standards of portfolio management (that the organization must embed across the programmes and projects) can be thought of as a system, with parts of it as processes that have standards embedded within the nature of those processes.

Good systems and processes have in-built measurement and control to monitor against deviation. Process control approaches are as equally applicable to a portfolio as to operational activities. Portfolios are managed through activities that need to be carried out in a defined way. Success is only achieved if the customers of the portfolio (the operations that will change) are fully satisfied with the result. In the programmes and projects within the portfolios the quality management process should provide the control to ensure customers are satisfied by the products and services that are their outputs. Asking the following questions may be helpful when assessing the level of success of the quality management processes used within the portfolio:

- Do we understand well the interdependencies inherent in a process?
- Can you see the integration and alignment of the processes that will best achieve the desired results?
- Are there structured approaches that harmonize and integrate processes?
- Is there clear understanding of the roles and responsibilities for achieving common objectives (and thereby reducing cross-functional barriers)?
- How well can we focus effort on the right processes?
- Can we take into account capability and resource constraints prior to action?
- Have we fully defined how activities should inter-operate to obtain desired results?
- Are we continually improving systems through measurement and evaluation?
- Have we established clear responsibility and accountability for managing activities?
- Do we know the interfaces of activities within and between functions?
- Are we focused on the factors that will improve activities of the organization?

The portfolio has a number of tools for ensuring the acceptable quality of the outcomes of the programmes and the outputs of the projects:

- **Portfolio Quality Management Strategy**
  The Portfolio Quality Management Strategy defines the activities for managing quality across the portfolio. It should also contain any of the individual programme's Quality Management Strategies, where there is a justified necessity for divergence from the Portfolio Quality Management Strategy. The portfolio may wish to give additional support for those programmes that need to implement a Quality Management Strategy that is divergent from the standards and controls of the Portfolio Quality Management Strategy.

  Programmes involving formal contracts with third parties for delivery of products or services to the programme will need to consider the relevant contractual requirements concerning quality management. Quality requirements specified in contracts should be consistent with the portfolio's overall Quality Management Strategy.

  For both those projects adhering to the Portfolio Quality Management Strategy, and those that need to implement a Quality Management Strategy that is divergent from the standards and controls of the Portfolio Quality Management Strategy, the strategy should list the quality activities, when these are triggered, a description of the quality assurance, review and control processes together with the roles and responsibilities of those taking these actions across the programme.

The Portfolio Quality Management Strategy provides input to the planning of the portfolio to ensure the required resources and time commitments are built into the programme and project plans. The Portfolio Quality Management Strategy is complemented by the Quality Schedule to ensure that the appropriate quality activities are carried out in the right order and at the right time.

- **Portfolio Quality Schedule**
  The quality schedule can be used to explain the arrangements for implementing the Portfolio Quality Management Strategy, and should include:

  - A plan of the activities required to implement the Portfolio Quality Management Strategy
  - Plans and dates for audits and reviews
  - The resources needed for the successful execution of specific quality activities.

A.4 ESTABLISHING AND RUNNING THE PORTFOLIO'S CONFIGURATION MANAGEMENT STANDARDS

Configuration management is a well-established discipline that ensures a set of components fit together to function properly as an assembly. The purpose of configuration management is to identify, track and protect the portfolio's assets (i.e. anything that is of material value to its success). These can be grouped as follows:

- The assets of the portfolio itself, for example the Portfolio Strategy
- Interfaces between the portfolio and the programmes and projects within the portfolio, for example progress reports
- Programme and project deliverables and outputs.

Portfolio information is a critical asset. This should include, for example, standardization of the information baselines that the programme and projects are to use. Baselines

inter-relate. If one document is changed, configuration management should help assess the impact on the others.

Success in a portfolio is often reliant on the satisfactory functioning of a combined set of programme and project outputs and operational functions. The failure of one component may mean failure of the whole assembly. If changed operations are depending on that complete assembly and if it malfunctions, then the desired improvements may well not be achieved, leading to possible failure for a large part of the portfolio.

The portfolio is in a special position of configuration management authority. Projects and programmes need effective configuration management for the items under the control of the projects and programmes, but they also need to deliver products into operational environments that will have their own configuration management requirements. The portfolio should:

- Direct programmes and projects as to the configuration management requirements that must be achieved operationally
- Be able to state some clear principles that must be followed
- Indicate specific configuration management standards that must be followed.

For these reasons it is important that portfolios have a process of ensuring that all individual components or sub-products of a complete system (the configuration) are identified, understood and maintained, with any changes to them assessed, tested and their release controlled.

There is a two-way relationship between quality and configuration management:

- Quality makes sure effective configuration management is in place
- Quality is dependent on configuration management, for example to make sure quality reviews are provided with the correct information.

A.5 STARTING PROGRAMMES

Starting programmes effectively with control and strategic alignment is a control activity of the Portfolio Office. The Portfolio Office should look to provide the Programme Manager with this support and control. A portfolio should have good knowledge about the overall requirements for each programme (from the Portfolio Schedule and to a lesser extent the Portfolio Plan) before the programme has started. The programmes in the portfolio should be started with a thorough brief that has had adequate input and review from the Portfolio Office to ensure necessary strategic alignment, visibility and control. The Programme Brief should:

- State the programme's objectives, scope, outcomes, constraints and interfaces
- Provide direction and clarity about how the programme will contribute to delivering against the Portfolio Strategy
- Define the authority delegated to the programme, with clarity about how and when it needs to escalate to the portfolio
- State how and in what format the programme will report progress to the portfolio
- Provide guidance on the standards to which the programme should conform through its management activities.

A.6 PROGRAMME CONTROL

The Portfolio Office should ensure that each programme adopts and adheres to the management processes of the portfolio, with clearly assigned responsibilities and owners. Programme governance should be formally integrated with portfolio governance to ensure the programmes remain aligned to the objectives of the portfolio.

The Portfolio Director and Portfolio Office should continue to guide the programmes, focusing on matters such as

programme interdependencies and the impact on programmes from strategic or portfolio risks and issues.

It may be advisable to periodically ask the programme's Senior Responsible Owners to assess their understanding of their relationship with the portfolio, with questions such as:

- How will your programme's outcomes contribute to delivering against the Portfolio Strategy?
- What benefits will the outcomes of your programme lead to?
- What is the enabling that your programme outcomes will need (if any) to deliver benefits?
- What other programmes are you dependent on to deliver your outcomes?
- What other programmes are dependent on your programme to deliver their outcomes?
- What contribution to delivering against the Portfolio Strategy will these other programmes make?
- What is the current state of these other programmes?

A.7 PROGRAMME AND PROJECT AUDITS, HEALTH-CHECKS AND REVIEWS

Audit is a generic activity, not one confined solely to the audit of financial accounts, and is often used to assess the management and conduct of a programme or project within the portfolio. Audit involves examination of the activities of a programme or project with the aim of determining the extent to which they conform to accepted criteria. The criteria may be internal standards and procedures or external codes of practice, accounting standards, contract conditions or statutory requirements.

Audit is about ensuring the programme or project is doing things right as defined in the portfolio's (and possibly its own) change standards, i.e. is it following the rules? However, it might be right to expect an audit to also check evidence that the programme or project is doing the right things (relative to its Business Case), that its progress so far is on track to achieving benefits and it is aligned to the organization's strategy. It is not unheard of for the audit to also assess the inherent achievability of the Business Case.

Programme or project audits may also consider any or all aspects of its management and delivery capability. While audits tend to focus on conformance and compliance, health-checks may be used as a programme assurance tool by senior managers to determine whether a programme should continue. Health-checks can also be used to provide an impartial view of a programme during its lifecycle to assess whether or not it will meet its objectives.

A.7.1 Value of review

Review is an important activity that is often forgotten or ignored. Without review, the findings of audits or other forms of assessment of the programmes and projects in the portfolio cannot be evaluated properly, and may well lead to ill-informed decisions and actions regarding the performance and direction of the portfolio.

Portfolio control and review activities include meetings between the:

- Portfolio Director and the Programme SROs, Portfolio Board Meetings
- Portfolio support team (e.g. those managing risk, benefits, dependencies for the portfolio) and the corresponding programme specialists or the Programme Manager
- The SRO and the Programme Manager, Programme Board meetings, Business Change meetings;

and any meeting where decisions are taken that affect the focus, success and delivery of the portfolio, including the effectiveness and efficiency of the programmes. These meetings should be set out in the quality schedules for the portfolio and the programmes.

A.7.2 Review focus

Review and assurance is more about ensuring the programmes and projects are doing the right things, for example as defined in the Programme's Blueprint and Programme Plan. It might be pertinent to require a review to also check evidence that the programmes and projects are doing things right, that the activities comply with the management strategies that are part of portfolio's change standards. Another focus of reviews should be to foster a culture of continuous improvement, supporting the idea of the portfolio being an evolving organization.

A.7.3 OGC Gateway Reviews

In the UK public sector many programmes are subject to the OGC Gateway Review 0. This strategic-level review provides assurance to the Programme Board that the scope and purpose of the programme has been adequately researched, that there is a shared understanding of what is to be achieved by the main players, that it fits within the department's overall policy or management strategy and priorities; and that there is a realistic possibility of securing the resources needed for delivery. The review will, in addition, examine how the work-strands will be organized (in sub-programmes, projects etc) to deliver the overall programme objectives, and that the programme management structure, monitoring and resourcing is appropriate. It is worth noting that OGC Gateway Reviews result in the production of a review report that is confidential between the review team and the SRO. The report is not intended for the Programme Board, although nearly all SROs share the findings with the board.

In short, the first OGC Gateway Review 0 aims to test whether stakeholders' expectations of the programme are realistic, by reference to costs, outcomes, resource needs, timetable and general achievability. Subsequent OGC Gateway 0 Reviews revisit the same questions to confirm that the main stakeholders have a common understanding of desired outcomes and that the programme is likely to achieve them.

There is high value in the portfolio using something akin to the OGC Gateway Review as check/confirmation that its programmes are both deliverable and aligned to the Portfolio Strategy. The cost and effort saved by refocusing or cancelling a programme that is no longer strategically aligned far outweighs the cost and inconvenience of the activity.

A.8 CONTROL OF PROCUREMENT, PARTNERS AND SUPPLIERS

Across a portfolio there may well be multiple suppliers and partners. The portfolio is the home for ensuring the application (and possible tailoring) of the organization's procurement and supplier management standards across the programmes and projects of the portfolio. Just as many operational parts of an organization depend on their suppliers providing goods or services that are fit for purpose, so too is a portfolio dependent on its suppliers. Quality in a portfolio also has to ensure that the suppliers deliver fit for purpose. A portfolio's suppliers are internal and external:

- Internal – for example, the organization's functions or business units providing resources and services
  - Here the principles of partnering, agreement and commitment will apply. For this to work, the business units and operational areas of the organization must have the visibility and understanding of the changes, and confidence in the deliverability, value, timeliness and resource cost of the changes to be able to make the commitments and plan accordingly

- External – for example, providers of temporary offices and infrastructure for the duration of a particular programme (it is here that procurement rules may need to be reviewed and tailored to ensure their application in a project-based environment)
  - Here the principles of clarity and ownership must apply. If the external supplier is to deliver or provide as expected, there must be an agreed understanding with the supplier.

An organization and its suppliers are interdependent and a mutually beneficial relationship increases the inclination of both parties to create greater shared value.

Benefits:

- Increased ability to create value for both parties
- Flexibility and speed of joint responses to changing market or customer needs and expectations
- Optimization of costs and resources.

Applying the principles of mutually beneficial supplier relationships typically leads to:

- Relationships that balance short-term gains with long-term considerations
- Pooling of expertise and resources with partners
- Identifying and selecting suppliers more effectively
- Clear and more open communication
- Sharing information and future plans, allowing better responses from both parties
- Establishing joint development and improvement activities
- Encouraging and recognizing improvements and achievements by suppliers.

Overview of the OGC's P3M3

B

Annex B: Overview of the OGC's P3M3

Table B.1 provides an overview of the OGC's Portfolio, Programme and Project Management Maturity Model (P3M3), which helps organizations to assess their current capability and determine their action plans for improvement.

Table B.1 Overview of the OGC's P3M3

Maturity	Project	Programme	Portfolio
Level 1 – initial process	Does the organization recognize projects and run them differently from its ongoing business? (Projects may be run informally with no standard process or tracking system.)	Does the organization recognize programmes and run them differently from projects? (Programmes may be run informally with no standard process or tracking system.)	Does the organization's board recognize programmes and projects and run an informal list of its investments in programmes and projects? (There may be no formal tracking and reporting process.)
Level 2 – repeatable process	Does the organization ensure that each project is run with its own processes and procedures to a minimum specified standard? (There may be limited consistency or coordination between projects.)	Does the organization ensure that each programme is run with its own processes and procedures to a minimum specified standard? (There may be limited consistency or coordination between programmes.)	Does the organization ensure that each programme and/or project in its portfolio is run with its own processes and procedures to a minimum specified standard? (There may be limited consistency or coordination.)
Level 3 – defined process	Does the organization have its own centrally controlled project processes, *and* can individual projects flex within these processes to suit the particular project?	Does the organization have its own centrally controlled programme processes *and* can individual programmes flex within these processes to suit the particular programme?	Does the organization have its own centrally controlled programme and project processes *and* can individual programmes and projects flex within these processes to suit particular programmes and/or projects? And does the organization have its own portfolio management process?

Table B.1 Overview of the OGC's P3M3 – *continued*

Maturity	Project	Programme	Portfolio
Level 4 – managed process	Does the organization obtain and retain specific measurements on its project management performance *and* run a quality management organization to better predict future performance?	Does the organization obtain and retain specific measurements on its programme management performance *and* run a quality management organization to better predict future programme outcomes?	Does the organization obtain and retain specific management metrics on its whole portfolio of programmes and projects as a means of predicting future performance? Does the organization assess its capacity to manage programmes and projects and prioritize them accordingly?
Level 5 – optimized process	Does the organization run continuous process improvement *with* proactive problem and technology management for projects in order to improve its ability to predict performance over time and optimize processes?	Does the organization run continuous process improvement *with* proactive problem and technology management for programmes in order to improve its ability to predict performance over time and optimize processes?	Does the organization run continuous process improvement *with* proactive problem and technology management for the portfolio in order to improve its ability to predict performance over time and optimize processes?

Common causes
of failure

Annex C: Common causes of failure

Experience has shown that there are common causes of failure wherever there is an initial drive for coordinated delivery of programmes and projects.

C.1 POORLY USED PROJECT AND PROGRAMME MANAGEMENT PROCESS

If the integration of the project and programme management process is inadequate or weakly implemented (as defined in the Change Delivery Framework), then the projects and programmes, individually and in aggregate, will not have the rigour and control that they need to be able to deliver against the expectations set out in the Portfolio Control Framework

C.2 WEAK GOVERNANCE STRUCTURES

Effective governance must integrate complete clarity about roles, responsibilities and authority to make decisions about the portfolio and its constituent programmes and projects. Problems with governance can occur in several ways:

- No agreed framework for decisions, so accountability is unclear
- Governance treated as solely for investment approval or audit
- Stakeholders excluded, or not committed, because of cultural barriers
- Too much complexity in decision gates
- Lack of clarity about how the governance framework should be applied.

C.3 COMPLEXITY IN APPROACH, PROCESSES AND TOOLS

Organizations that are new to portfolio management are often tempted to deploy complex software tools. The risk is that they are over-reliant on tools that may not produce accurate results; processes to manage the portfolio might not have been thought out and tested in practice before adding complexity. Software tools, in particular, may involve considerable cost and effort that could be better employed in embedding the portfolio management approach. The key, especially at the start, is to achieve the right balance of simplicity and rigour. A recommended approach in a complex organizational environment is to pilot the portfolio management processes before rolling out across the whole department.

C.4 INCONSISTENT APPLICATION OF SELECTION AND PRIORITIZATION CRITERIA

Every organization will recognize the problem of pet projects (those projects treated specially, not to have to conform to the standards and rules of the portfolio). The only way to resolve this is to develop selection and prioritization criteria that always apply to all programmes and their constituent projects, no matter who owns them. Even where a programme or project is mandatory, it must be able to demonstrate that it meets the selection and prioritization criteria set by the Portfolio Board/Portfolio Director. A culture of strong business case scrutiny will help.

There is also the situation where inconsistency is not deliberate. The underlying problem in this situation is that the information provided is inadequate or unreliable. Clear and simple standards for information reporting should be defined and applied.

C.5 LACK OF LEADERSHIP IN DIRECTING CHANGE

One of the highly publicized common causes of failure in programmes and projects is lack of commitment from senior stakeholders. At the portfolio level this is manifested as an unwillingness to make collective decisions about the portfolio.

Capability improvement initiatives are a related problem. It is important to aim for improvement, but not at the expense of focusing on improved strategic outcomes.

The solution is to make a clear separation between the primary need for leaders to take decisions focused on outcomes and the secondary need for their support in improving portfolio management processes (an enabler but not a substitute for leaders' decisions).

C.6 INADEQUATE MARKETING OF THE PORTFOLIO APPROACH

As with any change effort, the reasons for taking the portfolio approach must be communicated to stakeholders at the outset and thereafter. Typical problems include enthusiasm at the start, then less commitment because the benefits have not been sold to the stakeholder community. Conversely, initial resistance may never be overcome if the implementation of portfolio management is not managed as a change in its own right.

Visible leadership, with a champion for the change, and ongoing communication about the benefits being realized, provide the answer to the change problem.

Further information

Further information

The links and publications identified below will help you achieve a greater level of understanding of PRINCE2 and MSP, how to apply them effectively, and put you in contact with the rest of the PRINCE2 and MSP community.

PUBLICATIONS

- *Managing Successful Projects with PRINCE2*
  ISBN 9780113309467

- *Tailoring PRINCE2*
  ISBN 9780113308972

- *Business Benefits through Programme and Project Management*
  ISBN 9780113310250

- *People Issues and PRINCE2*
  ISBN 9780113308965

- *PRINCE2 for the Project Executive: Practical advice for achieving project governance*
  ISBN 9780113309672

- *For Successful Project Management: Think PRINCE2*
  ISBN 9780113310289

- *Managing Successful Programmes (MSP)*
  ISBN 9780113310401

- *For Successful Programme Management: Think MSP*
  ISBN 9780113310630

OTHER PUBLICATIONS OF INTEREST

- *Management of Risk: Guidance for Practitioners (M_o_R)*
  ISBN 9780113310388

WEB LINKS

- Best Management Practice Website – the OGC official umbrella site dedicated to making access to the guidance quick and easy, and providing support for all levels of adoption of the OGC Best Practice guidance.
  www.best-management-practice.com

- Official User Group
  www.usergroup.org.uk

- P3M3/P2MM models
  www.ogc.gov.uk

- P3M3/P2MM accreditation details
  www.apmgroup.co.uk

Glossary

Glossary

Activity

An activity is a process, function or task that occurs over time, has recognizable results and is managed.

Aggregated Risk

The overall level of risk to the programme when all the risks are viewed as a totality rather than individually. This could include the outputs of particular scenarios or risk combinations.

Assumption

A statement that is taken as being true for the purposes of planning a Project, but which could change later. An assumption is made where some facts are not yet known or decided and is usually reserved for matters of such significance that if they change or turn out not to be true then the project will need considerable re-planning. Examples of assumptions include:

- funding will be made available for national roll-out; or
- we will not need to procure web-hosting services.

Assurance

All the systematic actions necessary to provide confidence that the target [system, process, organization, programme, project, outcome, benefit, capability, product output, deliverable] is appropriate. Appropriateness might be defined subjectively or objectively in different circumstances. The implication is that assurance will have a level of independence from that which is being assured.

Baseline

Reference level against which an entity is monitored and controlled.

Benefit

The measurable improvement resulting from an outcome perceived as an advantage by one or more stakeholders.

Benefits Management

The identification, definition, tracking, realization and optimization of benefits usually within a programme.

Benefits Realization

For projects, the practice of aligning the outcome associated with the project with the projected benefits claimed in the Business Case.

Benefits Realization Manager

An optional role within the organization that is responsible for maintaining a permanent 'centre of expertise' in benefit realization within the organization, providing objective challenge of benefits, dependencies, measures, targets and the programme's approach to benefit realization.

Benefits Realization Plan

A complete view of all the Benefit Profiles in the form of a schedule.

Best Practice

A defined and proven method of managing events effectively.

Blueprint

A model of the business or organization, its working practices and processes, the information it requires and the technology that will be needed to deliver the capability described in the Vision Statement.

Business as usual

The way the business normally achieves its objectives.

Business Case

The justification for an organizational activity [strategic, programme, project, operational] which typically contains costs, benefits, risks and timescales and against which continuing viability is tested.

Business Change Manager

The role responsible for benefits management, from identification through to realization and ensuring the implementation and embedding of the new capabilities delivered by the projects. Typically allocated to more than one individual. Alternative title: 'Change Agent'.

Change Delivery Framework

The standardization of change activity across the portfolio's programmes and projects consisting of process descriptions, deliverables and role descriptions.

Change Manager

Reports to the Business Change Manager and may operate at a project level to support benefits realization, focusing on the realization of a particular benefit.

Checkpoint

A team-level, time-driven review of progress, usually involving a meeting.

Configuration Management

Technical and administrative activities concerned with the creation, maintenance and controlled change of configuration throughout the life of a product.

Corporate Governance

The ongoing activity of maintaining a sound system of internal control by which the directors and officers of an organization ensure that effective management systems, including financial monitoring and control systems, have been put in place to protect assets, earning capacity and the reputation of the organization.

Corporate Portfolio

The totality of the change initiatives within an organization; it may comprise a number of programmes, stand-alone projects and other initiatives that achieve congruence of change.

Exception

A situation where it can be forecast that there will be a deviation beyond the tolerance levels agreed between Project Manager and Project Board (or between Project Board and corporate or programme management, or between a Team Manager and the Project Manager).

Expected Value

This is calculated by multiplying the average impact by the probability percentage.

Exploitation

A risk response for an opportunity. Exploitation refers to changing an activities scope, suppliers or specification in order to achieve a beneficial outcome.

Gateway Review/s

Independent assurance reviews that occur at key decision points within the lifecycle of a programme or project.

Governance

The functions, responsibilities, processes and procedures that define how the programme is set up, managed and controlled.

Government Policy

The translation of a government's political priorities and principles into programmes and courses of action to deliver desired changes.

Highlight Report

Time-driven report from the Project Manager to the Project Board on stage progress.

Leadership

Leadership is the ability to direct, influence and motivate others towards a better outcome.

Opportunity

An uncertain event that could have a favourable impact on objectives or benefits.

Outcome

The result of change, normally affecting real-world behaviour and/or circumstances. Outcomes are desired when a change is conceived. Outcomes are achieved as a result of the activities undertaken to effect the change. In a programme, the outcome is the manifestation of part or all of the new state conceived in the Blueprint.

Output

The tangible or intangible product resulting from a planned activity.

P3M3

OGC's Portfolio, Programme and Project Management Maturity Model.

Phase

A part, section or segment of a project, similar in meaning to a PRINCE2 stage. The key meaning of stage in PRINCE2 terms is the use of management stages, i.e. sections of the project to which the Project Board only commits one at a time. A phase might be more connected to a time-slice, change of skills required or change of emphasis.

Plan

A detailed proposal for doing or achieving something detailing the what, when, how and by whom.

Policy

A course of action (or principle) adopted by an organization. A business state of intent, setting the tone for an organization's culture.

Portfolio

All the programmes and stand-alone projects being undertaken by an organization, a group of organizations or an organizational unit.

Portfolio Board

The head committee of the organization's portfolio management. Is responsible for the portfolio coming into existence and ensuring that the portfolio aligns with the organization's strategy.

Portfolio Control Framework

Comprises the Portfolio Strategy, Portfolio Plan and Portfolio Schedule.

Portfolio Director

The Portfolio Director is accountable to the Portfolio Board for the day-to-day performance of the portfolio and its delivery against the Portfolio Strategy. The Portfolio Director must have the seniority, authority and large-scale change expertise to provide appropriate leadership and guidance to the Portfolio Board.

Portfolio Management

The corporate, strategic-level process for coordinating successful delivery across an organization's entire set of programmes and projects.

Process

That which must be done to bring about a particular result in terms of information to be gathered, decisions to be made and results to be achieved.

Product

An input or output, whether tangible or intangible, that can be described in advance, created and tested. Also known as an output or deliverable.

Programme

Temporary flexible organization structure created to coordinate, direct and oversee the implementation of a set of related projects and activities in order to deliver outcomes and benefits related to the organization's strategic objectives. A programme is likely to have a life that spans several years.

Programme Assurance

Independent assessment and confirmation that the programme as a whole or any of its aspects are on track, applying relevant practices and procedures, and that the projects, activities and business rationale remain aligned to the programme's objectives (see also Gateway Review).

Programme Board

A group that is be established to support the SRO to deliver the programme.

Programme Management

The coordinated organization, direction and implementation of a dossier of projects and activities that together achieve outcomes and realize benefits that are of strategic importance.

Programme Manager

The role responsible for the set-up, management and delivery of the programme. Typically allocated to a single individual.

Programme Office

The function providing the information hub for the programme and its delivery objectives; would provide support for more than one programme

Programme Organization

How the programme will be managed throughout its lifecycle, the roles and responsibilities of individuals involved in the programme, and personnel management or human resources arrangements.

Programme Risk

Risk concerned with transforming high-level strategy into new ways of working to deliver benefits to the organization.

Project

A temporary organization that is created for the purpose of delivering one or more business products according to a specified Business Case.

Project Approach

A description of the way in which the work of the project is to be approached. For example: Are we building a product from scratch or buying in a product that already exists? Are the technology and products that we can use constrained by decisions taken at programme level?

Project Brief

Statement that describes the purpose, cost, time and performance requirements/constraints for a project.

Project Executive

The single individual with overall responsibility for ensuring that a project meets its objectives and delivers the projected benefits. This individual should ensure that the project or programme maintains its business focus, that it has clear authority and that the work, including risks, is actively managed. The Executive is the chairperson of the Project Board, representing the customer and owner of the Business Case.

Project Initiation Document (PID)

A logical document which brings together the key information needed to start the project on a sound basis and to convey that information to all concerned with the project.

Project Issue

A term used to cover any concern, query, Request for Change, suggestion or off-specification raised during a project. It can be about anything to do with the project.

Project Management

The planning, monitoring and control of all aspects of the project and the motivation of all those involved in it to achieve the project objectives on time and to the specified cost, quality and performance.

Project Manager

The person given the authority and responsibility to manage the project on a day-to-day basis to deliver the required products within the constraints agreed with the Project Board.

Project Plan

A high-level plan showing the major products of the project, when they will be delivered and at what cost. An initial Project Plan is presented as part of the Project Initiation Document. This is revised as information on actual progress appears. It is a major control document for the Project Board to measure actual progress against expectations.

Project Support

An administrative role in the project management team. Project Support can be in the form of advice and help with project management tools, guidance, administrative services such as filing, and the collection of actual data. The provision of any Project Support on a formal basis is optional. Tasks either need to be done by the Project Manager or delegated to a separate body and this will be driven by the needs of the individual project and Project Manager.

Quality

The totality of features and inherent or assigned characteristics of a product, person, process, service and/or system that bear its ability to show that it meets expectations or stated needs, requirements or specification.

Quality Assurance

Independent check that products will be fit for purpose or meet requirements.

Quality Management System

The complete set of quality standards, procedures and responsibilities for a site or organization.

Quality Review

A quality review is a quality checking technique with a specific structure, defined roles and procedure designed to ensure a product's completeness and adherence to standards. The participants are drawn from those with an interest in the product and those with the necessary skills to review its correctness. An example of the checks made by a quality review is: 'Does the document match the quality criteria in the Product Description?'

Risk

An uncertain event or set of events which, should it occur, will have an effect on the achievement of objectives. A risk is measured by a combination of the probability of a perceived threat or opportunity occurring and the magnitude of its impact on objectives.

Risk Appetite

An organization's unique attitude towards risk taking which in turn dictates the amount of risk that it considers is acceptable.

Risk Assessment

The identification and evaluation of risks.

Risk Management

The systematic application of principles, approach and processes to the tasks of identifying and assessing risks, and then planning and implementing risk responses.

Risk Register

A record of identified risks relating to an initiative, including their status and history.

Senior Responsible Owner

The single individual with overall responsibility for ensuring that a project or programme meets its objectives and delivers the projected benefits.

Senior Supplier

The Project Board role that provides knowledge and experience of the main discipline(s) involved in the production of the project's deliverable(s). Represents the supplier interests within the project and provides supplier resources.

Senior User

The Project Board role accountable for ensuring that user needs are specified correctly and that the solution meets those needs.

Specification

A detailed statement of what the user wants in terms of products, what these should look like, what they should do and with what they should interface.

Sponsor

The main driving force behind a programme or project.

Sponsoring Group

The main driving force behind a programme who provide the investment decision and top-level endorsement of the rationale and objectives of the programme.

Stage

A stage is the section of the project that the Project Manager is managing on behalf of the Project Board at any one time, at the end of which the Project Board wishes to review progress to date, the state of the Project Plan, Business Case and risks, and the next Stage Plan in order to decide whether to continue with the project.

Stakeholder

Any individual, group or organization that can affect, be affected by, or perceive itself to be affected by, an initiative [programme, project, activity, risk].

Strategy

Approach or line to take, designed to achieve a long-term aim. Strategies can exist at different levels in an organization – in MSP there are corporate strategies for achieving objectives that will give rise to programmes. Programmes then develop strategies aligned with these corporate objectives against particular delivery areas.

Supplier

The group or groups responsible for the supply of the project's specialist products.

Threat

An uncertain event which could have a negative impact on objectives or benefits.

Tolerance

The permissible deviation above and below a plan's estimate of time and cost without escalating the deviation to the next level of management. Separate tolerance figures should be given for time and cost. There may also be tolerance levels for quality, scope, benefit and risk. Tolerance is applied at project, stage and team levels.

Tranche

A group of projects structured around distinct step changes in capability and benefit delivery.

Transfer

A risk response for a threat whereby a third party takes on responsibility for an aspect of the threat.

Transformation

A distinct change to the way an organization conducts all or part of its business.

User(s)

The person or groups responsible for the supply of the project's specialist products.

Index

Index

Note: Page numbers referring only to figures and tables are followed by (Fig) and (Tab) respectively.